# Interculturality and the Political within Education

This innovative book problematises the internal relationships within and between the intercultural and the political in education. It engages in a critical dialogue with current practices and discourses, and the focus on 'the political' offers an alternative trajectory to explore interculturality within education.

Drawing on international research and consolidated with the application of top interdisciplinary theories in the field, Dervin and Simpson alert us to the current dangers of treating interculturality loosely in education. The authors engage in a dialogue to encourage readers to examine the meaning of interculturality and the state of research in education today, suggesting that we move beyond merely rehearsing theories, concepts and methods. More importantly they urge researchers, teachers and students to question Western-centric ideologies of interculturality.

*Interculturality and the Political within Education* is a must read for those who are dissatisfied with current intercultural research and education. It will be of great interest to researchers and students of the philosophy of education and those interested in the contemporary debates concerning ideologies, definitions and ownership of interculturality.

**Fred Dervin** is Professor of Multicultural Education at the University of Helsinki, Finland. He also holds distinguished professorships in Australia, Canada, China, Luxembourg, Malaysia and Sweden.

**Ashley Simpson** is a Lecturer in Language Education at the University of Edinburgh, UK.

# Routledge Research in Education

This series aims to present the latest research from right across the field of education. It is not confined to any particular area or school of thought and seeks to provide coverage of a broad range of topics, theories and issues from around the world.

Recent titles in the series include

**The Role of Research in Teachers' Work**
Narratives of Classroom Action Research
*Lesley Scanlon*

**Community-based Media Pedagogies**
Relational Practices of Listening in the Commons
*Bronwen Low, Paula M. Salvio, and Chloe Brushwood Rose*

**Designing for Learning in a Networked World**
*Edited by Nina Bonderup Dohn*

**Personal Narratives of Black Educational Leaders**
Pathways to Academic Success
*Robert T. Palmer, Mykia Olive, Joycelyn Hughes, Chase Frazer, and Barbara Boakye*

**Building Trust and Resilience among Black Male High School Students**
Boys to Men
*Stuart Rhoden*

**Interculturality and the Political within Education**
*Fred Dervin and Ashley Simpson*

For more information about this series, please visit: www.routledge.com/
Routledge-Research-in-Education/book-series/SE0393

# Interculturality and the Political within Education

**Fred Dervin and
Ashley Simpson**

LONDON AND NEW YORK

First edition published 2021
by Routledge
2 Park Square, Milton Park, Abingdon, Oxon, OX14 4RN

and by Routledge
605 Third Avenue, New York, NY 10158

*Routledge is an imprint of the Taylor & Francis Group, an informa business*

© 2021 Fred Dervin and Ashley Simpson

The right of Fred Dervin and Ashley Simpson to be identified as authors of this work has been asserted by them in accordance with sections 77 and 78 of the Copyright, Designs and Patents Act 1988.

*Trademark notice*: Product or corporate names may be trademarks or registered trademarks, and are used only for identification and explanation without intent to infringe.

*British Library Cataloguing-in-Publication Data*
A catalogue record for this book is available from the British Library

*Library of Congress Cataloging-in-Publication Data*
A catalog record for this book has been requested

ISBN: 978-1-138-59999-4 (hbk)
ISBN: 978-0-367-76767-9 (pbk)
ISBN: 978-0-429-47115-5 (ebk)

Typeset in Times New Roman
by Apex CoVantage, LLC

# Contents

# Introduction

In Spring 1865, while visiting his family, Karl Marx filled out a questionnaire entitled *Confessions*, which was very popular in Victorian England. The questionnaire contained items such as "The quality you like best", "Your aversion", "Your favourite colour of eyes and hair". For the item "Your motto", he wrote down in Latin "De omnibus dubitandum" [doubt everything] (Singer, 1980: 93). This motto applies to what we are attempting to do in this book about the omnipresent, yet problematic, notion of *interculturality*.

Interculturality is a word of consequence, a word that matters in education, although it might be used as a mere 'stop-gap' at times.

All things 'intercultural' in research and education have spread around the world in different waves. To start with, it is important to say that the idea of interculturality is not a new 'thing'. The phenomenon and the education that goes with it (*how to prepare people to meet other people*) have occurred throughout history under different guises. In research and education, it found an official voice in the 20th century. In the 1950s American diplomacy led the way with the work of the anthropologist E. T. Hall who set a stepping stone by providing American diplomats with training in intercultural communication. The business world followed suit, first in the 'West'. Interculturality has become a global industry today (e.g. intercultural consultancy). Education has also witnessed some kind of 'intercultural revolution', especially since mass migration to the Western world and the increased internationalisation of higher education.

Discussions of civil rights, social justice, racism, 'clash of civilisations', orientalism, etc. over the past decades have also had to do with interculturality. We should remember, however, that although we use the word *intercultural* in this book, many other (similar) initiatives have emerged over the past decades, under different labels: multicultural, transcultural and the fashionable term 'global' as in 'global citizenship' and 'global competence'.

Things have changed over the decades, and many ideas from the past 70 years have been questioned – although they can still be identified in some books, research papers and curricula. Amongst the critiques about past perspectives on interculturality, different kinds of -*isms* have been under attack: Euro- and Western-centrism (the influence of Western and European ideologies on how we deal with interculturality), culturalism (culture as the explanation for everything in interculturality), essentialism (people's essence as the only explanatory force for what they do and say), East-West-ism, etc. More postmodern, so-called non-essentialist, perspectives have appeared to do away with some of these issues. Some other approaches try to include voices that have been silent/silenced in intercultural scholarship and to open up dialogues about the notion of interculturality. For example, a recent textbook for English majors, published in China, promises just to do that. Written by Yuxin, J., Byram, M., Xuerui, J., Li, S. and Xuerui, J. (2019), *Experiencing global intercultural communication: Preparing for a community of shared future for mankind and global citizenship* attempts a pluralistic approach to 'global intercultural communication'. However, we feel that it does not do justice to real global perspectives. As such, although some elements of 'Chinese culture and philosophy' are included *here and there* in the book, it is hard to see how they work with the canonical 'Western' intercultural knowledge that fills the book. The imbalance between 'Western' and other knowledge is obvious for example in the collection of about 50 quotes that appear throughout *Experiencing global intercultural communication*. Less than five quotes are from/about China and a few quotes from other parts of the world (e.g. India and Turkey). The rest are from British and American scholars from the broad field of intercultural communication education. Ideologically, this makes such a potentially important initiative still dominated by what has been critiqued about scholarship on interculturality.

## Why did we write this book?

For Althusser (1965: 67), the way we deal with a specific issue relies on a range of concepts which guide the questions we ask, and therefore the answers we provide. Our main motivation in writing this book is to send the message that we need to treat the notion of interculturality very carefully. We know this complex field very well, having been involved and engaged with top scholars and participated in many international research projects on intercultural issues. What is more, our research and teaching experiences in places like China and Russia have alerted us to the current dangers of treating interculturality loosely. What we have witnessed in these contexts is 'desperate' teachers and researchers being forced implicitly to teach about interculturality from American textbooks and to research the notion following e.g. American and British models of *intercultural competence* (a central concept in the field of interculturality). This often leads to students merely 'parroting' these theories, models, concepts and methods, without realising that they do not always make sense in their own context and in their languages. The answers they receive to their questions about interculturality are thus (wrongly) 'governed' by concepts that are provided to them in intercultural communication education. We have witnessed the same in Finland where some scholars and students rehearsed 'by rote' ideologies passed onto them by American multiculturalists such as James Banks or the European Union and the Council of Europe – two important marketers of everything 'intercultural'.

People tend to recycle, rehearse, apply, judge their students and/or research participants against these ideologies, without a hint of criticality. This is why we felt the need to examine the current situation and to launch debates concerning ideologies, definitions and ownership of interculturality. We suggest breaking the dominating habitual ways of thinking about and 'doing' interculturality but also to reconfigure current 'critical' discussions of the notion (to which e.g. Fred has contributed in the past, see Dervin, 2016).

**Book structure**

Amongst the six chapters that compose the book, five were written in the form of dialogues. We wanted our readers to witness the way scholars unthink concepts, notions, epistemologies, methods and assumptions related to interculturality and renegotiate them together. Each chapter corresponds to a question about interculturality: *(Chapter 1) What to make of the notion of interculturality? (Chapter 2) Who was influential in the ways we understand interculturality? (Chapter 3) How does intercultural research and education influence experiences of interculturality? (Chapter 4) Can we prepare/get prepared for interculturality? (Chapter 5) What is the state of research on interculturality today?* We each take the floor to provide answers and then explore our differences and similarities. We also ask questions to the reader at the end of each chapter. The final chapter entitled "The intercultural is always ideological and political" is a response to a response to one of our critical articles about a reference framework of interculturality – disguised under the label of 'democratic culture', produced by a European team led by two white British 'native speakers' of English. We use this chapter as a concrete illustration of how the political (and ideologies of not being ideological about interculturality) and interculturality are enmeshed in education. The conclusion to the book offers a clear and succinct summary of what to take away from this book and covers three aspects that we feel are essential: conceptualising, researching and preparing for interculturality.

## Working method

Our working principles are as follow:

1. Systematically, we examine the 'travel' of the words that are used in English and other languages to deal with interculturality. There is a tendency to use notions and concepts in English without questioning their meanings in this global language – and other languages – as if words were just mere equivalents. We argue that this increases the gap between the powerful voices that impose them and the voiceless who just have to accept them and use them to survive if they wish to e.g. publish in international journals ('governed' by the powerful voices) and/or to be allowed to speak at international conferences. In their volume entitled *Words in Motion*, Gluck and Lowenhaupt Tsing (2009: 11) maintain:

> Words stabilize our understanding. They allow us to insert ourselves into discourses, institutions, and social relations. . . . Our focus is how words and worlds are made at different scales, ranging from particular class niches and political campaigns to transnational realignments of culture and power. This task involves watching words move across space and time.

Take for example the simple word of *a thing* in English. According to Merriam-Webster (www.merriam-webster.com/dictionary/thing), a thing is "1. an object or entity not precisely designated or capable of being designated use this thing; 2. an inanimate object distinguished from a living being". When we are taught to write, we are asked not to use this 'nothing word' since it is not exact enough and has no 'being'. Interestingly, in the Chinese language, *a thing* translates as 东西, which refers to East and West. In this language, a thing is thought of in terms of relations and movement between these two positions, rather than hinting at the *not-being*. This might have an influence on the way different people see their relation to the word and to the realities this very word represents.

In the book, we include archaeologies, discussions of untranslatable words as much as possible to emphasise the need to be critical of recycling words from English. This will allow us to become aware of the ideologies that such words impose on the users and listeners. This will also allow us to revise some notions and assumptions related to interculturality.

2. Our book relies on genuine interdisciplinarity. Dealing with interculturality requires awareness and use of updated knowledge from other fields of scholarship. Too often in education, old-fashioned terms, rejected in the field where they originally appeared, are used to look into certain phenomena. We must do an archeology of all the concepts that we use in the field of

interculturality and look for alternative ways of thinking about it. By doing so, we can rewrite our imaginations about interculturality. In this book, we use knowledge from philosophy, sociology, anthropology, psychology and cultural studies (amongst others). Input from literature, the graphic arts, the performing arts and music also enrich our discussions. We believe that it is only through such interdisciplinary engagement that interculturality can be problematised. We should not create boundaries between the different fields of knowledge and the arts since they all can contribute to renewing the notion.

3. Having had the opportunity to explore the way interculturality is taught and researched in different parts of the world, we note that the overall emphasis is still on individuals interacting with each other, with an exclusive focus on each of these individuals. As such, their relations or what they do and co-construct together are rarely taken into account – all seems to relate to the 'self'. For example, those researching the concept of intercultural competence will tend to 'test', 'analyse', 'observe', 'report on' one interactant's skills, ignoring the fact that their skills relate to a specific context and to the interlocutors' identity, behaviours and intertextuality (e.g. how much they remind them of another social being). Even more important, the influence of research, (global) administration, (global) politics, the economy and the media on how people interact with each other, what they (don't) say or do, is systematically ignored to focus on e.g. stereotyping, individual racism and discrimination. In this book, we open up these discussions to include all these aspects in the way we problematise interculturality.

We hope that this book highlights the urgency to revise our often simplistic or mechanic ways of thinking about interculturality and that it can lead to changes in the way the notion is used around the world. There is a need to make the notion more intercultural itself by including alternative voices about it. An increased awareness of the economic and political determinants of intercultural knowledge and practice in education is also crucial more than ever.

# 1 Characterising interculturality

**(F.D.)**

There seems to be a current interest in trying to (re-)define or (re-)negotiate the meaning of interculturality. In early 2020, I was contacted by two different research groups (China and Germany) that were recruiting global experts for Delphi studies on intercultural competence – a concept often considered as central for interculturality in education. In the studies, multiple rounds of questionnaires were sent about the meaning of intercultural competence, aggregated and shared with all of them after each round. Both research groups wanted to come up with one definition of the concept. I declined to participate when I saw the list of researchers who were to be involved – the 'usual suspects' of interculturality.

The Austrian writer and journalist Karl Kraus (1874–1936) summarises well the problem we face when we try to define the notion of interculturality when he asserts (2014: 64): "He masters the German language – that is true of a salesman. An artist is a servant of the word". Some people ('salesmen') seem to be able to define interculturality easily by making lists of characteristics of this phenomenon and the competences that people should have when they deal with it (*they can do 'interculturalspeak', i.e. speak about interculturality in a somewhat automatic, acritical way*), while others ('artists') find it too complex a notion to be able to demarcate and characterise it in words. The former rarely question the definition of interculturality that they give – and do not allow others to do so. They are entitled to define it in a certain way by e.g. listing (sub-)competences because of their symbolic power (e.g. white, British, professor) and of the support they receive from important institutions such as the Council of Europe or the United Nations Educational, Scientific and Cultural Organisation (UNESCO). Some 'salesmen' of interculturality, usually from outside the 'West', even support these powerful Western salesmen to protect their own privileged position in their own (unprivileged) space and to play the role of knowledge gatekeeper amongst their own (unprivileged) people.

Although I have been writing about the notion for over 15 years, I place myself increasingly in the category of 'artists'. I ask many questions about interculturality, but I rarely have any answers. I don't think we need to have answers. As such, I often feel my endeavours resemble those of Kuafu (夸父), the giant in Chinese mythology who wished to capture the sun, following it from the East to the West, and who, after drinking all the rivers and lakes crossing his path, died of dehydration. I believe that trying to capture interculturality is always bound to fail. Every attempt that I have made to define, tackle or deal with interculturality, I feel I have failed. I actually reject some of the work that I have written about the notion. And I think we should all go through this process: if part of the work on interculturality is about reflexivity and criticality, scholars and educators should voice and put on paper their dissatisfaction and frustration with the way interculturality is discussed and delimited. I am always wary of scholars who rehash the same ideas (and ideologies as we shall see later) about interculturality, even when they claim to 'revisit' what they wrote 15 years ago.

The notion of interculturality is everywhere, sometimes, it 'hides' under other labels such as *multicultural, transcultural, polycultural, crosscultural* and even *global*, which may mean the same or something else.[1] In the 21st century, there seems to be a global search (and care?) for this notion by decision-makers, educators, researchers (amongst others). Today's globalisation – note: I write *today's* since globalisation has been with us for centuries, see Hansen (2010) about globalisation in the year 1000 – seems to urge us to deal with interculturality, or maybe, if I rephrase what I just wrote, *we are made to believe that globalisation forces us to become 'intercultural'*. In the 19th century work of epic poetry entitled *Kalevala* (1894), compiled by philologist Elias Lönnrot (1802–1884) from Karelian and Finnish oral folklore and mythology, one finds a magical artefact (the Sampo), that some of the characters wish to discover. The Sampo is meant to bring riches and good fortune to its holder. However, nobody seems to know what it is: *A world pillar? A compass? A Byzantine coin die?* I argue that interculturality (and its companion terms) is in fact a Sampo: everybody longs for it, but nobody really knows what it is. Actually, some people (decision makers and/ or scholars working with and for them) might know what they mean by it, as they often manipulate the notion for their own (economic and political) benefits and to impose ideologies onto others: students, teachers and researchers.

In general, I would say that the notion means either too much or too little. What is more, although there can appear to be a smörgåsbord of perspectives on interculturality around the world, some specific Western-centric ideologies dominate the way the world thinks about it. These ideologies are promoted by scholars who have a lot of symbolic power, represented by their status, institutional belonging, identity as 'English native-speakers', publications in top journals, editorship of book series with top publishers, etc. We could venture a comparison with the Austrian philosophical writer Robert Musil (1880–1942), who wrote about philosophers that they are "despots who have no armies to command, so they subject the world to their tyranny by locking it up in a system of thought" (1996: 272).

In order to try to position my own thinking about interculturality, I wish to start by explaining what I think *it is not*. In what follows, I list ideas that are part of a global *doxa* (taken-for-granted, unquestionable 'truths') about interculturality and create common beliefs and self-evident arguments about it. The reason why I want to start by elements that I reject are: 1. We need to drain the swamp of clichés about interculturality in research and education that were created since the 1950s. 2. As an ideological construct, interculturality cannot but be tackled without considering how it is understood and used in relation to the space of discourses and realities of capitalism as well as global neoliberal politics – aspects that must be discussed openly, questioned and/or rejected.

1   Interculturality is always a viewpoint since the quality of *a thing, a person or a relation* being intercultural relies on the one who labels them as such – which may not be shared by the observed, other participants and/or observers. As philosopher Louis Althusser (2017) puts it: *the concept of the dog does not bark*. So, in a sense, **anything/anyone that is described as intercultural is not necessarily intercultural**

2   **Interculturality is not about 'cultures meeting and/or clashing'.** This has been, until now, the dominating view on what interculturality is about in the world. The overuse and abuse of the tired concept of *culture*, which I claim is a remnant of another era (18th-century Europe), has attracted too much attention in research and education about interculturality. The concept means too much or too little to be useful today. The ideas of 'cultural difference', 'knowledge about other cultures', 'culture shock[2]', 'the clash of cultures' all represent, *willy-nilly*, caricatures and simplifications that, I maintain, have neither intellectual merit nor 'value neutrality' (Weber, 1949). Maybe as much as Dabashi (2015: 25) believes that a notion such as Orientalism has become "disposable knowledge", since it appears not to be "predicated on any enduring episteme" (a specific system of understanding) today, the same could be said about culture. The aforementioned ideas can also easily remove the complexity from the human, superimposing the mechanical on the living as French philosopher Henri Bergson (1859–1941) would have it (1911). The mechanical biologises culture, i.e. gives the impression and illusion that 'culture' is biological: cultural habits are often described as 'natural', 'part of our/their DNA',

which people cannot (easily) change. By so doing, hierarchies are created between different cultures, with the one operating these comparisons often placing themselves on top of a cultural ladder of 'more civilised', 'politer', 'more punctual', 'more hardworking', 'quieter', etc. In research and education, discourses about culture are systematically expressed and used by people who have the power to dictate such discourses the way they wish to dictate them (often speaking for and over others) and impose them through their teaching and research to individuals, whose status is inferior (students, teachers), and who are made to believe that by possessing knowledge about the Other, they can 'govern' them. The theoretical glaciation of culture to deal with interculturality is often put forward by (supranational) institutions such as the United Nations Educational, Scientific and Cultural Organisation (UNESCO), the European Union (EU) and the Council of Europe and passed down to others by scholars and educators with symbolic power, who are e.g. involved in the projects these institutions sponsor and promote. EU projects on interculturality, for example, have clear ideological bases: boosting European identity (i.e. the identity of a neoliberal economic and political institution, the EU). Therefore, the way interculturality is constructed in such projects systematically relates to and rehearses EU ideologies, which seems to prevent alternative intercultural ideologies to emerge. I have been involved in many such projects where dominant, EU-friendly 'research' on interculturality, where the concept of culture is central were obviously favoured. Another problem with the concept of culture is that, in some contexts, it is a mere substitute for other concepts that are not used (Eriksen, 2001). For instance, in some European countries, the concept of *race* cannot be 'voiced'. Instead, scholars and educators refer to *ethnicity* and/or *culture*, while promoting e.g. anti-racism. By its flexibility and somewhat apparent apolitical connotations, the concept of culture can, however, lead to racist/discriminatory judgements about others, while pretending to discuss e.g. 'cultural difference' about time use and/or honesty. I suspect that a lot of work on interculturality has led learners to have certain racist thoughts that they may not have had before they studied the notion (e.g. Hofstedian[3] notions of power distance, indulgence, etc. See: www.hofstede-insights.com/product/compare-countries/). In that sense, interculturality as a notion can be a chameleon, a reptile that is able to change colours. As we shall see later, this is not a problem as such. However, it becomes a problem when it gets stuck on one colour ('one model'), when it changes colours and leads to (further) racism, discrimination, unequal treatment, or when it pretends to change colours

3   In terms of education for interculturality, the idea that the awareness and knowledge of other cultures can help us either reduce or remove stereotypes is strong and yet somewhat awkward. There is a problem with the overemphasis on stereotypes. *First*, stereotypes are unstable elements that can reemerge at any moment even when we believe that we have 'suppressed' them. They relate to our emotions and to a part of us that makes us think irrationally about what we experience. So, stereotypes can never really be 'destroyed' – it is mere wishful thinking. *Second*, if one can suppress one stereotype, another one will appear straight away about a different aspect of who we are and who the other one is (for example, we might want to suppress our belief that all Finns are honest, but then we might start believing that they are all dishonest). There is a saying in Chinese that expresses this problem very well: 是坚持政治解决冲突的方向。世界上热点问题不少，按下葫芦起了瓢 (*"Just when you press the gourd into the water, there floats the gourd ladle"*). A gourd is a kind of pumpkin with a hard skin. One cannot submerge a gourd entirely as one side of the fruit will always float on the surface of water. The same goes for stereotypes; they can never be 'drowned', tackling one only leads to finding another one. **Interculturality is not about suppressing or pretending to overcome stereotyping**

4   Similarly, **interculturality is not about adapting to another culture.** It is not about becoming a *facsimile* of the Other (and vice versa). And it is not about what some scholars refer to as 'cultural shifting' (shifting or switching languages, behaviours or gestures according to interlocutors). I believe that the saying "When in Rome, do as romans do" has no place in interculturality. It has now become a xyloglossia (from the Greek for *wooden language*), a vague and ambiguous saying that diverts attention from the salient issues of interculturality. The focus on difference in discourses of adaptation still represents a strong bias. As I was writing these lines, I received a message about a training session on 'Chinese culture' at a British university that was described as follows: "Are you interested in gaining a deeper understanding of how Chinese culture differs from yours? . . . In this seminar [the speaker] will provide us with a means to not only identify and analyse cultural differences, but also to reconcile them". I believe that this illustrates well a differentialist bias as well as a push towards 'adapting to another culture'. However, the very word interculturality contains the prefix *inter-* which refers to *between, mutually, reciprocally, together* – and not *unilateral, affecting one party only*. Interculturality should be the result of negotiations, reflexive and critical dialogues – not mere *copy-paste*

5   About dialogue, **interculturality is not represented by the typical questions that have accompanied intercultural encounters since the**

**beginning of the 18th century**, based on the modern ideologies of the nation-state, national identity and national language. As such, 'Where are you from?'[4] (and for some people, the systematic follow-up question, 'where are you *really* from?'), 'What is your culture?', 'What is your mother tongue?', are questions that do not allow interculturality to happen. They create, *nolens volens*, hierarchies rather than encounters. As such, Chinese essayist, editor, journalist and translator Xiao Qian (1910–1999) wrote the following about his time in England: "A person abroad quite often is not simply himself (sic), but a reflection of his country's position in the eyes of others. One is made to bear not just one's own character but one's national character as well" (1990: 78). The aforementioned questions, although they might appear 'obvious', 'a nice way to get to know each other', are in fact political questions that we may want to leave to the police or border control services. For many people, answering these questions requires to make choices in terms of what to answer. Depending on the interlocutor and the context of interaction, this might lead them to have to make choices between various identities or even to refrain from telling the 'truth' about their origins for fear of discrimination and/or stereotyping. People should have the freedom to choose: 1. not to answer these questions and/or 2. not to tell the 'truth'. Like many people in the world, I have experienced this kind of 'police inquiry'. For example, in Italy, I remember having dinner with a group of European scholars specialising in 'intercultural issues' and being 'harassed' by one of them repeatedly about my 'real' identity for 20 minutes ("Fred, where do you really come from?"), while I was clearly not willing to talk about my family history in front of strangers. This led me to reveal one dark side of my family history as a way of sending the message that answering such questions is never easy. I remember being upset and traumatised by this 'bullying' from people whom I thought would refrain from doing this. Recently, I was also asked if I am 'ethnically Finnish' when I proposed alternative views on Finland's happiness and 'miraculous education'. Another person asked me 'in what language – note the singular – I dream in' when I told them that I speak several languages on a daily basis. All these questions represent attempts at finding a simple answer, that is, in fact, not complex ('the living') but mechanical and singular. At the same time, one can easily see that these questions are both political and related to capitalist evaluations: *What is my worth in the eye of the Other? Am I a real Finn (can this be validated and thus validate the authenticity of my discourse about Finnish happiness and education)? Can I really navigate between six different languages?* In brief: *What is the value of my passport and language skills in the eye of the Other?* The playwright

Eric Mok (2020) puts it nicely when he reflects on people playing what he calls the "where are you from game": "'Oh, that's where you are from?' Like they have won some quiz or something". That game is that of validation. As a middle-aged scholar and educator, with symbolic power, it should be somewhat easy to respond to such 'police inquiries' since I have had years to prepare and strengthen my counter-discourses. However, think about those who don't have the chance and opportunities that people like me have to question such painful episodes. I am thinking of a so-called Black 'migrant-background' child in a Finnish school that I visited some months ago, who was repeatedly put back in his 'non-Finn' position by his teachers when he refused to play the 'migrant-background' game (he had a Finnish passport and had never been outside the country)

6    Finally, I would say that **interculturality does not correspond to the concepts and notions that are currently used globally to research and/or teach about it.** Some examples (in alphabetical order and randomly): *collectivism-individualism, culture (shock), democracy, intercultural citizenship, intercultural competence, open-mindedness, respect, tolerance.* Although these terms might be used worldwide to talk about interculturality ('intercultural ready-to-think'), they might 1. mean different things to different people, 2. may not have the same connotations in different languages and 3. negate *interculturality* by having been imposed onto the rest of the world by 'Western' ideologues

We were writing this book in summer 2020, during the so-called COVID-19 crisis, which, beyond the vast sanitary and social issues, created – or rather amplified – many crises of interculturality. Symbolically, one of the major figures of interculturality, Geert Hofstede (1928–2020) passed away at the very beginning of the crisis. Not that I would want to make it a symbol of the end of an era, but his somewhat *culturalist* (placing [national] culture at the centre of every single explanation of what interculturality is about) and *essentialist* (reducing people to a narrow and limiting view of their identity) 'theories' and 'methods' of interculturality were questioned straight from the beginning of the crisis in February 2020. Discourses on cultural models of how different people behave and think across the globe were put into question since people started behaving in somewhat similar irrational ways (e.g. panic buying, toilet paper/hand sanitizer hoarding, non-respect of lockdown, critiques of those in power, see Dervin et al., 2020). What also became obvious about the way the crisis was handled by different governments was that the survival of capitalism was deemed implicitly more important than saving lives. As a consequence, certain culturalist explanations about collectivism and individualism that we had been made to believe in were shattered. If we take the example of Finland at the time of writing – we were both 'stuck' in the country for months – no official decision had been made about recommending wearing face masks, although the discussion started six months earlier in the media.

Repeatedly, the authorities have claimed that face masks are not useful and that they should not be made compulsory – using at times the sole voice of 'Finnish researchers' to support their claims, as a way of protecting themselves. In reality, at the beginning of the crisis up until May 2020, masks were very difficult to come by in Finnish pharmacies and supermarkets. Once they became available, the price of one single mask ranged from 1–7e (up until the end of August 2020). The discussion about Finns not being willing to wear a mask to protect their freedom and trust for each other (or other kinds of culturalist arguments) has overshadowed this non-negligible economic aspect of the discussions. Repeatedly, throughout the crisis, accusations were made about some countries (or even cities or regions) in terms of how badly they had managed the crisis, about hygiene, about people's seriousness, etc. Interestingly, the targets of these accusations changed as the virus travelled. Of course, the case of China is of interest here. From the beginning of the crisis, many Western countries started attacking the Middle Kingdom about just everything (beyond the virus): Hong Kong, Xinjiang, Inner Mongolia, 5G and Huawei, spying, etc.[5] Many Chinese experienced racism on Western streets as a consequence of these attacks. All of these disrupted somewhat the way we have been thinking about interculturality as they have unveiled what has mattered the most (but that had not been discussed in the open in research and education on interculturality): the obsession with the faulty concept of culture and stereotypes in dealing with interculturality has tended to divert our attention from or make us blind towards other important realities and aspects of interculturality. As such, very little attention has been paid to how economic domination, business-driven politics and capitalistic mistreatment of the Other intervene systematically in intercultural encounters. Interculturality is situated within specific contexts governed by the economy, political power struggles and contradictions.

Now it is time for me to reveal one of the most important points that I wish to make about interculturality: the notion is governed by a wide range of ideologies around the world – and the same applies to its companion terms such as *multicultural, polycultural, transcultural, global,* etc. It means that the notion might be understood, defined, problematised and discussed in different ways in diverse contexts. This should rejoice us because it means that there are multiple voices and thus views to be heard about interculturality. So, when we talk to someone about interculturality it is important to know from which perspective – and thus which ideology – they are talking about interculturality – as much as I need to be aware of my own ideology:

*What concepts and notions do we use?*, *What is the archeology of these terms around the world?*, *Who proposed them/introduced them to discuss interculturality?*, *What political motivations are behind them?*, etc. In a TV programme from 2015, the British actor Stephen Fry was asked what he would say if he was confronted by God one day. His answer, I believe, is very relevant for us here: "Which god are you?". So, every time we face discussions, discourses, views and opinions about interculturality, we need to ask a similar question: *Which interculturality are you/am I?*

Things would be satisfactory if there were a real smörgåsbord of perspectives of interculturality from which we could choose. Nevertheless, this is not the case, because amongst all these voices, some of them are much 'louder' than others, supported by global systems of economic-political dominating institutions such as top world universities (e.g. in the United Kingdom [UK] and the United States [US]), supranational institutions (the UNESCO, the Council of Europe, where the same white English-speaking scholars dominate), the world of academic publishing (journals and books in which the dominating voices get to be published and quoted), etc. Looking at the fields of research that deal with interculturality, ideologies developed in Europe and the US tend to dominate because of the system of academic supremacy that they have established in the world. Although ideologies might differ within the 'West', there seem to be some leading theories, discourses, concepts and methods, that I have mentioned before. These are problematic for several reasons. And the COVID-19 crisis has helped me to open my eyes to these issues.

I would now like to take a detour via the important concept of *ideology* to be able to position further my thinking about interculturality. In order to do so, I will refer to a French Marxist philosopher, Louis Althusser (1918–1990).

Going back to the COVID-19 crisis, it is clear that what the crisis has revealed is that interculturality has to do first and foremost with the inequality created by political and economic relations and corporate powers. Thus, the notion cannot be approached, thought of and/or conceptualised without reflecting on these aspects. Anyone who says that interculturality has nothing to do with capitalist ideologies, is being ideological. Interestingly the *prêt-à-penser* (French for *ready-to-think*) discourses on the problematic and yet resistant concept of intercultural (communicative) competence nearly systematically refers to two adverbs that relate to capitalism, production and control: "effectively" and "appropriately" (see e.g. Deardorff's model). These two adverbs reveal ideologies related to practical purposes, success, productivity, usefulness and benefits. However, interculturality should not and cannot be treated as a product or a service that one can/should control and/or get benefits from (from an ethical perspective). In her critical work on management methods in today's companies, the French sociologist Danièle Linhart (2015) describes what she calls a "human comedy" whereby a pseudo-humanist approach of happiness and care is performed around the idea of competence, while preventing employees from being critical of what they are supposed to be doing. I believe that current models of intercultural (communicative) competence do the same to students: they 'indoctrinate' them with specific ideologies, which they are urged to take for granted and refrain from questioning. I believe that authors of these models would claim that their work is not ideological.

Now let me talk about this very concept of ideology. For Althusser (2001: 45), "Man (sic) is an ideological animal by nature". Because of that, people systematically misrepresent and are made to imagine the reality of the socioeconomic relationships in which they live. As such, they are 'drowned' in a flow of discourses, images and ideas in which they grow up, live, think, interact, create, etc. These become the obvious, the aforementioned *doxa*: they are just taken for granted and hardly questioned. However, according to Althusser, they represent illusion on reality (2011: 29).[6] The reason why this occurs is because they are determined by a given society's production relations embedded in the complex network of economic relationships, from which *no one can escape* (neither the dominant nor the dominated). The imaginaries that people use to represent the reality are influenced first and foremost by what Althusser calls ideological state apparatuses (2001), which determine a system of production relations in which people live. These include two kinds of apparatuses: 1. repressive ones which function by violence (e.g. courts, the police, prisons, the army); 2. ideological state apparatuses such as religion, education, politics, trade unions, the media, the arts. These function by ideology and tell us to think and act in the interests of the economic dominance of the ruling class. In addition to these apparatuses, which may give an illusion of localism ('nation-states'), it is obvious that, today, global ideological aparatuses have an influence on us. For example, in terms of education, through the influence of institutions like the UNESCO and the Organisation for Economic Cooperation and Development (OECD) (which are all embedded in modes of capitalist production), certain perspectives are favoured: e.g. happy and fun learning, autonomous learning, global competence. There are no 'neutral' discourses about education, especially as they serve the very purpose of corporate power, while at the same time giving an illusion of autonomy, agency, freedom and open-mindedness. People have no choice but to submit freely to all these apparatuses in the interests of the economy through the education they receive. A selected case of privileged people may occupy different positions in relation to these ideologies: producers, exploiters, repressors, ideologisers and even scientists in service of apparatuses (Althusser, 2001: 38). For example, a scholar producing a model of intercultural competence for a global ideological apparatus (e.g. the Council of Europe) contributes to spreading particular ideologies (e.g. Eurocentric views on democracy and human rights, derived from the 'Enlightenment') that are embedded in politics and the economy. These ideologies cannot but distort the existing relations of production and make people believe in imaginary relationships instead of their real relations (Althusser, 2001: 38). While these are presented as ideas that lead to some form of intercultural dialogue, they do not allow any alternative ideology on these issues to compete with them. They become part of a system of ideological intimidation ("so you question the whole idea of human rights?"; "human rights are non-negotiable"; "don't throw the baby with the bathwater" when someone wants to do away with the ideological concept of culture) and contribute to political and economic domination of the West (Althusser, 2001: 49). So how we should 'do' interculturality is then an 'order' from the apparatuses that these scholars work for as consultants, disguised under discourses of research and the 'aura' of famous scholars who tend to be white, American and British English-speakers.[7] Instead of making changes in structural economic inequality (which governs any intercultural encounter), for example, the individual is asked to change, to adapt and to follow what has been decided for them. The way they see interculturality, embedded in the discourses backed by the apparatuses, becomes the global norm for how individuals should meet and, in a way, incapacitates (etymologically "to deprive of natural power") them from thinking. Some agents of the apparatuses even modify their discourses around interculturality to 'sell' it outside their own context. This is the case for example of the Reference Framework of Competences for Democratic Culture, developed by the Council of Europe for use in "primary and secondary schools and higher education and vocational training institutions throughout Europe as well as national curricula and teaching programmes" (see: www.coe.int/en/web/campaign-free-to-speak-safe-to-learn/reference-framework-of-competences-for-democratic-culture). Ashley and I have written extensively about the problems posed by this Framework (Simpson & Dervin, 2019). When he presented the Framework in China, one of its authors (a white English native-speaking scholar), had removed the word 'democratic' from the name of the model he had himself proposed – the model on his PPT was photographed (and maybe used?) by hundreds of Chinese scholars during the event, without them realising that, ideologically, it was 'very' Eurocentric.

Currently, the dominating ideologies of interculturality lead to unquestionable mottos such as: "you must be tolerant", "you must respect other cultures", "you must believe in democracy and human rights". These are all problematic since (again!) 1. They can be polysemic in different languages; 2. They do not seem to contribute to dialogue and/or negotiations (reminder:

the *inter-* of interculturality); 3. They relate to ideologies invented in 18th-century Modern Europe, thus, disregard the contribution of other parts of the world in the way one reflects on interculturality; 4. The responsibility for interculturality is left in the hands of the individual who is kept busy imagining themselves and others (trying to figure out what their culture is) and made to feel guilty about their stereotypes and 'personal' racist thoughts. What people actually need is to be trained to look at inequality, divisions and hierarchies created by and through ideological apparatuses. 5. These ideologies do not correspond to the harsh reality of many people's experiences (poverty, economic discrimination, structural racism, systematical political exclusion rather than *disrespect for their culture or respect of democracy*). I am thinking of two examples from Finland:

1   During the COVID-19 crisis, the state ideological apparatuses discovered that some Somali communities in Helsinki had been infected by the virus in larger numbers than other communities. In their first explanations, the media made use of culturalist ideologies to explain: "Somalis are collectivistic; families have many children, unlike Finns". References to linguistic issues were also made: "we need to hire interpreters to help them understand the situation, their Finnish is not good enough". Alternative explanations were never mentioned. For example, one could discuss the fact that many Somalis are segregated in small, city-owned flats outside the city centre, where space is limited and thus it is difficult to do social distancing; many work in the low-paid service industries and had to continue to e.g. deliver meals to customers (without face masks) to earn a living. These all have to do with economic aspects, rather than 'culture'.

2   During the crisis, the media also 'discovered' that many so-called minorities were mistreated and underpaid in the service industries (e.g. cleaners) – something that had been discussed by the Finnish media for years. The Prime Minister of the time, Sanna Marin, made a statement explaining that she would not let this kind of discrimination and mistreatment happen. However, a week later, her government begged the Thai authorities to send seasonal workers to pick berries, since very few Finns were interested in doing it themselves. The working conditions for these Thai workers have been criticised over the years for doing exactly what the media had discovered about the mistreatment of 'minorities'. Again, discourses of social justice, good intentions and 'shock at inequality', although this time not hidden under culturalist discourses, can hide other truths (corporate power again).

There is another concept that Althusser (2001) uses which can help us problematise what Apparatuses do to interculturality (and the 'specialists' who work for them): *interpellation* (calling out to someone). For the philosopher, by *interpellating* individuals with these ideologies (e.g. believe in and do not question cultural difference, democracy, human rights), ideological practices become natural and obvious ways of being and behaving – even if they might contradict people's experiences and encounters. By being forced, pressured and rewarded to think and reject identities, relationships and connections to institutions, for example, people become *agents of ideology*. At the same time, apparatuses impose subjectivities on individuals ("you must be a global citizen"; "you must be open-minded") while encouraging them to think that these subjectivities can be self-generated (Althusser, 2001). One example to illustrate: I have met many doctoral students around the world who use old-fashioned and extremely Western-centric theories and scholars (e.g. Bourdieu, E. T. Hall) who are unable to explain why they have chosen them and who seem reluctant to question them since "I am only a student" (heard repeatedly from some students around the world). What we don't realise is that these imposed subjectivities 'install' meaning systems within people that urge them to accept and/or celebrate capitalist exploitation (without realising it). One last example about interpellation which relates to a book project: A colleague had been asking repeatedly how an edited volume that I was working on was advancing (he needed the publication for promotion – a very capitalist but now normal approach to research). A few days ago, he sent me another email, in which he did not mention the book, but was inquiring about how I was doing, updating us about his family (whom I had never met) and ending with the now common order of "Stay safe". I realised while reading the message that there was a hidden message behind the nice words and 'care': *How is the book progressing?* Although the email might have passed as a kind act of intercultural dialogue, it was clear that the real intention of the message was the 'care' for the colleague's promotion – rather than my health and well-being. Ideology of interculturality works this way: on the surface we can have polite, tolerant and caring discourses, while, underneath, hides the pressure of capitalist exploitation. *The market before encounters.*

Of course, in some other fields of research or societal contexts, some people try to subvert or contest systems of domination. However, as far as interculturality is concerned, being in research, education or daily life, many of the imposed subjectivities (*be interculturally competent, autonomous, tolerant*, etc.!) are rarely put into question.

Interestingly, I recently became aware of the confusion – and manipulations – that the interpellation of these ideologies of interculturality can create in students' views on interculturality when I interviewed some Chinese students who had taken courses on interculturality at Chinese universities. The courses were all taught by Chinese teachers, who were forced to use textbooks produced in the US and the UK. When confronting their own experiences of interculturality and the 'knowledge' they had acquired in the courses, it became clear that the courses had imposed a set of ideologies on the students (e.g. cultural differentialism, culture shock, individualism-collectivism, the need for intercultural communicative competence *à la* Byram), which became part of their constructed views on encounters. When they spoke about interculturality in general, after the course, all these ideologies were omnipresent. On the other hand, when they discussed real encounters that they had had, these ideologies were marginal in their discourses and alternative ideologies such as *similarities in terms of generation and cultural preferences* were used by the students. When they seemed not to have been able to understand aspects of these encounters, they would throw in the course ideologies, often unconvincingly. No mention of economic or political influences was made by the students. Like most courses of interculturality around the world, the course objectives had been cleansed of such essential elements. Finally, none of the students questioned the ideologies imposed onto them during the course. This is how ideology works, and it is easy to see the problems with this. Maybe students of interculturality should reject this regime of explaining/understanding interculturality to allow alternatives to emerge. But would they have enough power to do so?

And now, finally, we come to how I see and understand interculturality, after these very long – and yet necessary – detours. At least now, the reader should know *what I don't think interculturality is* and that Althusser's theories of ideology are central in my understanding of it.

**Interculturality is a wide range of ideologies found around the world.** These ideologies are passed onto people through different apparatuses, which they mostly accept – with a few rejecting them, for example, in education. This smörgåsbord of ideologies is, however, dominated by some Euro-/Americano-centric ideologies, often promoted by global ideological apparatuses in e.g. education (The Council of Europe, the OECD). All these ideologies cannot but relate to political and economic relations and corporate power.

So, as a complex and ideological construct, **interculturality must first be approached from a dialogical approach.** Whenever I come across the word, or when I meet someone for whom interculturality seems to matter, I need to ask myself: *What ideologies are being used to deal with 'us' and 'them' by myself and others? Do they clash or concur? What does and does not seem to count as interculturality? Are we aware of these ideologies? Where do they come from? Do we agree with them? If we disagree, can we renegotiate them and (maybe) lower our chances of being dominated? What place might personal experience have in relation to these ideologies? Do they confirm and/or contradict them?* Nelson (2020: 6) defines the task of what he calls intercultural philosophy to "reveal the multiperspectivality and multi-directionality of thinking". Trying to answer these questions corresponds to revealing these important aspects of interculturality.

Following the Croatian philosopher Srecko Horvat's (2019) idea about what he calls *poetry* (which could be interculturality in a sense), the way we approach interculturality should undermine the dominant system in which everything is measured. In intercultural encounters, everything is calculated and quantified without us realising. We ask ourselves and each other indirectly: *What is our worth?* (skin colour, nationality, number of 'prestigious' languages spoken, coupled with social status), *Are we worth our encounter?* and *What benefits can we get from our encounter?* ("I have a friend from Japan", "I can practice my English with you"). Cultures, languages and identities coupled with social and economic status, and other important aspects of valuing people socially, do have an influence on how we meet the Other. So, maybe, interculturality could be about trying to do away with these 'surface' elements and to dig into the underworld of encounters. Following Karl Kraus (2014: 34), I would argue that we need to re-imagine the world: "it is necessary to strengthen the real backbone of life, the imagination". To do so, we need to dig under the surface of what interculturality is presented/constructed to be.

Obviously, this is a difficult task, as one cannot approach an object without being ideological. Claiming that we can do away with ideologies would also be very ideological. If we reimagine, we re-ideologise. We always start somewhere, be it our perceptions of own intercultural experiences and/or the influence of multiple apparatuses. Yet, what interculturality should lead us to do is to open up to a wider range of ideologies so that we can look at intercultural issues from multiple perspectives, and, possibly, have more opportunities for (re-)negotiation and choices. The more perspectives, the better to get out of our small ideological bubbles.

I will now take one last detour, via music this time. Speaking about his piece *Improvisation for snare dream* (1987), the composer John Cage explains that this work is a form of *composed improvisation*. This oxymoron is based on what he calls *chance procedures*, which entitle the performers to improvise around two pages of the score provided by Cage. The score includes rules with which to design a structure for the improvisation. The performer writes all kinds of answers to a question on pieces of paper and then picks them out of a hat while performing. I believe that interculturality should be viewed as composed improvisation too. When we meet someone or discuss interculturality, we need to start from some basic information about the diverse ways we see and 'do' interculturality (but also from questions of inequality, politics, the place of the economy in our everyday lives and encounters). As we interact, we take some of these ideologies out of the hat and improvise encounters and discussions around interculturality with the aim to question and explore as many alternative ideologies as possible with others. Through this dialogue, I believe we can have the impression to be freed from dominating ideologies and to open up to other ideologies – and thus other worlds, other ways of being made to think about the world.

In my work with my friends and colleagues Mei Yuan and Sude at Minzu University of China in Beijing, we have noticed that our students may experience this *improvised composition* much more than students in other universities in China (and in other countries). Minzu University is a so-called minority institution in Mainland China that hosts students from the 56 official Minzus of China (Minzu is wrongly translated as *minority* in English because it gives a wrong impression of the economic-politico-linguistic reality of China). In our work on interculturality with students in education, we noticed that they navigate through various ideologies when they talk about encounters and dialogue (amongst others): so-called 'Western' ideologies (tolerance, respect, open-mindedness) with references to Byram and Deardorff, but also, and most importantly, the university ideological position towards intercultural dialogue ("Knowledge corresponds with actions"; "Diversity in Unity"), Chinese political discourses about Minzus ("Harmony without uniformity"), as well as more localised Minzu discourses ("we Hui[8] learn the language of others to facilitate understanding") (see Yuan et al., 2020). Reviewing this smörgåsbord with the students, they realise how they have been influenced by different voices, but also how incompatible some of these ideologies "pushed down their throats" are. For instance, the ideology of 'intercultural citizenship' as promoted by e.g. Byram was mentioned repeatedly by the students. When we asked them to define it and explain how it fits in with other ideologies, the students were shocked to realise that what hides behind this ideology (disguised as a necessary concept to be 'good' at interculturality) are imposed subjectivities based on Eurocentric views of democracy and human rights (feigning that politics and the economy do not matter), which may not necessarily be 'compatible' with their other ideologies. What the students do with these, is, in a sense, their problem, however we believe that they need to be aware of this range of ideologies, their origins, how they relate to systems of domination, their polysemy and potential compatibility.

Figure 1.1 summarises my discussions of interculturality in this first chapter.

**Dominating ideologies to question**

Interculturality is neutral/natural as a notion
It is about the meeting/clash of cultures

Suppressing and/or pretending to overcome stereotyping
Adapting to other cultures
Becoming a facsimile of the 'other' (and vice versa)

**Looking into the smörgåsbord of ideologies**

Deconstructing the dominating ideologies (supported by global systems of politico-economic dominating institutions)
Identifying their orders, imposed (inter-)subjectivities and ideological intimidation

Opening up to alternative ideologies (localised/silenced in global research/educational worlds)
Looking at intercultural issues from multiple perspectives, and, possibly, have more opportunities for (re-)negotiation and choices

**Moving beyond**

"Which interculturality are you?"
"Why do we meet this or that way?"

Reimagining while being aware of re-ideologisation
Composed improvisation

*Figure 1.1*  Dealing with the smörgåsbord of interculturality

**(A.S.)**

Interculturality is neither a fixed state nor is it singular. It includes the processes of being and becoming and relates to how we understand who we are and our environment. Interculturality is the dynamic actioning between the self and others. The notion corresponds to the plain across, and within, which dialogues between the self and other are performed, negotiated and co-constructed. The dialogues between the self and the other are continuous and always in the making. These movements are simultaneously external (with others) and internal within the self (the others contained within us – our behaviour, actions, utterances).

In thinking about what interculturality means, we arrive at the Deleuzian notion of *univocity*. The French philosopher Gilles Deleuze (1925–1995) argues, "if Being is the unique event in which all events communicate with one another, univocity refers to both what occurs and what is said" (Deleuze, 1990: 180). Univocity refers to the identity of the 'noematic attribute'. In other words, the perceived is an intentional correlate of the act of perceiving. For Deleuze, sense in univocity does not exist outside the proposition which expresses it, and it is attributed to the thing. It is the event expressed by the verb.

This relationality between event and sense has been misinterpreted as the self interacting with referential objects (words, icons, signs, symbols). Often this has meant that the field of intercultural communication has misconstrued these referential objects as 'culture'. This externalisation of the self-other relationship neglects the internal dialogues of how the self comes into being and through such interactions. When referential objects (words, icons, signs, symbols) are conceptualised normatively – as fixed, static norms – this means they cannot be problematised nor contested. Such normativity denies the plurality of meaning and identity co-construction. Either the self violates the other, the self violates self or the other violates both itself and the self.

The (potentially) destabilising multi-directional synthesis of interculturality reminds me of a quote from the Russian philosopher Nikolai Berdyaev (1874–1948): "thinkers who devote themselves to epistemology seldom arrive at ontology" (Berdyaev, 1960: 1). Epistemology here refers to theories of knowledge while ontology to the nature of being. Berdyaev's quote provokes important questions for us to think about: Has interculturality (and the field of intercultural communication education generally) become fixated on finding epistemological answers to ontological questions? Or, why is it easier to find epistemological answers about interculturality (e.g. why people from one context act or behave a certain way) rather than problematising ontological questions?

Many postmodern criticisms of interculturality (and intercultural communication education generally) involve criticisms of hyper-relativism (only judge people according to their 'culture') and the infinite polysemy of meanings, concepts and inter-subjectivities (how people co-construct who they [think] they are) found about the notion. These criticisms for some still remain too discomforting, this can be bore out of the fact that 'old', 'culturalist' models are still very popular within the field (e.g. Ogay & Edelmann, 2016). Notwithstanding the fact that there have been a number of intercultural initiatives recently that have countered postmodern interpretations of intercultural communication for being too 'other-centred' as they negate the self's interests and desires, I would reject this distinction as the self is not simply biometrically opposed to the other – beings are multiple and different, they are always produced by a disjunctive synthesis, and they themselves are disjointed and divergent – this is also the same for the other.

Interculturality is ontology. Interculturality is a continual analysis, method and thesis of our being and belonging. There is a metaphor in Russian philosopher and literary critic Mikhail Bakhtin's (1990) work for interculturality (1895–1975): there is no alibi in Being (ne-alibi v bytii [не-алиби в бытии]). *One has no moral alibi*: one cannot escape neither one's own singularity nor one's unique place. It is on this non-alibi in being that the duty to act is based.

The Russian word *postupok [Поступок]* does not translate wholly to the word *act* in English. *Postupok* comes from the Old Russian noun *postup [поступ]*, "movement, action, act" (Sreznevskiĭ, Materialy, 2:1270) and, finally, the verb *stupat [ступать]*, "to walk, pace". Etymologically, *postupok* thus means "the step one has taken". *Postupok* is thus a reflexive and ontological overture that requires understanding the steps the self takes in conjunction with the other. The act (*postupok*) an individual takes is ethically determined by the relationality of the self-other relationship. The ethical ground is determined by the Russian word *svoboda*. The Russian term *svoboda [свобода]* (freedom) comes from the Slavic possessive pronoun *svoj [свой]*, which means belonging to the person and is rendered, depending on the context by "(my, your, his, our, your, their) own"" (Vasylchenko, 2014: 1105).

Vasylchenko (2014), argues,

> Svoboda reveals its structure in the novels of Dostoyevsky, whose characters are perpetually in intimate confrontations with Others (drugoj [другой], derived from drug [друг], "friend товарищ"), representing the entirety of the universe. The character must choose between the caritas of total responsibility for oneself and the universe, on the one hand, and the total diabolical destruction of "everything is permitted" (vsedozvolennost' [вседозволенность], derived from volja), on the other.
>
> (Vasylchenko, 2014: 1106)

The ground of *svoboda* is thus the relation between self and others, through co-being and co-existence, and ultimately all objects that relate to interculturality. It is on that structure that the free act *(postupok) [поступок]* is ultimately based. There is thus no alibi in interculturality because there is no alibi in Being.

In interculturality, one cannot transcend into another Being (Bakhtin calls attempts to do this as the work of an imposture), no other being can act or think for us in that moment – no one can think, see, hear, taste, feel what we do, our Being becomes irreducible to no other. The non-alibi in Being means we are continually obligated towards a reciprocal relationship with the other, and with others. It is on this non-alibi in being that the duty to act is based. That which can be done by me can never be done by anyone else. The uniqueness and singularity of present-on-hand Being is "compellently [sic] obligatory" (Bakhtin, 1990). Interculturality is thus concerned with problematising and understanding the being-event *(bytie-sobytie) [бытие-событие]* the world of the intersubjective event, our co-being, our common existence and our co-existence as human beings.

Let's take the following question as an example to illustrate how the free act *(postupok)* *[поступок]* is ultimately based. In [intercultural] encounters, we are often asked: *Where do you come from* (note, that this can be code for, why are you here?)? Perhaps the question is a false question/way of thinking. Why? Because it assumes that people are free to make that choice and will thus act upon that choice.

Perhaps this question should be broken down into the following sub-questions: *What if the act has already been predetermined and decided for both the self and other (by social, economic, political, educational forces, ideologies, etc.)? What if the act contains no choice at all? What if neither subject can exert any free will over the act or of being intercultural?*

There is a false assumption here: that we are free to be or act interculturally.

The act of whether you decide to reply truthfully, to lie, or act as an imposter in answering the question is irrelevant – it is about understanding and tracing the processes that lead to this situation in understanding how and why this question is being asked and how and why I am choosing to answer the way I am. *Postupok* enables one to ask both the self and the other, "How did we reach this act?"

This is a reflexive movement for both the self and others because the etymology of the word *Postupok* designates 'the step one has taken' (past tense) – we have already taken acts which predetermine where we are or where we will be going, so the task is to retrace our steps through our acts *[postupki]*.

In the example, we have already predetermined how we will answer the question or how we will choose not to, the ethical movement thus involves continually questioning one's position in relation to *postupok* and that of the other. Perhaps, part of the ethical dimension also involves what needs to be changed, how, and for what purpose, to result in different acts *(postupki)* or outcomes.

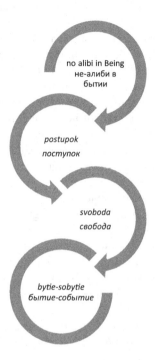

*Figure 1.2*  An alternative sense of interculturality

There is thus no alibi in interculturality because there is no alibi in Being. The act is still an act in itself – as are human beings (we cannot escape who we are, we have no alibi in being). This is not a void of emptiness and nothingness. On the contrary, it is where realities (people, ideas, notions, ideologies) collide.

Figure 1.2 shows how Mikhail Bakhtin's central idea of 'no alibi in being' works hand in hand with three other aforementioned notions (*postupok, svoboda* and *bytie-sobytie*), to create an alternative sense of interculturality:

## [Synopsis]

In this first chapter, we have discussed how we perceive and understand interculturality. Our answers clearly show how we situate ourselves at moment X – spring/summer 2020 in the middle of the COVID-19 crisis, which was an eye opener for us as it unveiled issues that were there before, but that the crisis amplified. Our readers should bear in mind that scholars and educators working on interculturality must change and shift between influences and ideologies – and discuss these movements openly in their work. What is more, for us, researching and educating for interculturality is not catechism (religious instruction), where people are given lists of 'invisible orders' on how to behave and to think about 'good' and/or 'bad' interculturality.

The danger of this catechism resembles what, in the Greek and Roman legend, Midas experienced when he was rewarded for a good deed by being able to turn anything he touched to gold: when the King wanted to eat, his food also became gold and thus he nearly starved to death.

What this first section also shows is that we are both influenced by different and yet complementary figures at the time of writing: Althusser and Bergson (Fred), Bakhtin and Dostoyevsky (Ashley). In the next chapter, we review the different thinkers who have helped us to tackle interculturality over the years.

It is obvious that our ways of conceptualising and critiquing interculturality are complementary. While Fred focused on the macrolevel of politics (and the embedment of research in it), Ashley discussed interculturality at the microlevel of interpersonal dialogue. In what follows, we summarise the main points made by the two of us and how they work hand in hand.

## Macrolevel (research embedded in politics)

### *Becoming aware of ideological intimidation*

1  Anything/anyone that is described as intercultural is not necessarily intercultural
2  The notion of interculturality means too much or too little
3  Research on interculturality is still dominated by Western ideologies (e.g. *culturespeak, tolerance, respect* and focus on *stereotypes*)
4  Issues of inequality, economic domination, business-driven politics, and capitalist mis/treatment of individuals are ignored, hidden in beautified discourses of social justice, democracy, tolerance
5  Global systems revolving around politico-economic dominating institutions give 'invisible' orders as to how to deal with interculturality ('effectively' and 'appropriately')

## Microlevel (personal dialogue)

### *Combating imposed intersubjectivities*

1  At the interpersonal level, interculturality is based on (endless) negotiations, reflexive and critical dialogues. The very word interculturality contains the prefix *inter-* which refers to *between, mutually, reciprocally,*

*together.* The dialogues between the self and the other are thus continuous and always in the making. However, the false assumption that *we are free to be or act interculturally* is omnipresent in research and education (amongst others)

2    a) There is a need to move beyond the imposture of *transcending into another Being*: no other being can act or think for us in moments of encounters. b) The political must be considered as acknowledging the permanent co-existence and irreducibility of antagonistic forces inherent between us

3    At the interpersonal level, interculturality could be understood as a reflexive and ontological overture that requires understanding the steps the self takes *in conjunction with* the other. The act (*postupok*) of interculturality is ethically determined by the relationality of the self-other relationship

4    Those who meet interculturally need to renew the questions they ask themselves and each other. Instead of the typical inquiries of, *Where do you (really) come from?* and *What is your mother tongue?*

- *Why are we speaking like that to each other? Why do we ask these questions (Why do we answer in such ways)?*
- *Why do we value each other this or that way?*
- *Why are we asked indirectly/guided to do this?*

**[Going further]**

Readers might want to consider asking themselves or others the following questions to continue reflecting on how they understand interculturality:

- *What concepts and notions do you use when you think of and 'do' interculturality?*
- *What is the archeology of these terms? Who proposed them/introduced them to discuss interculturality?*
- *What political motivations are behind them?*
- *Can you recall examples of intercultural encounters for which you can clearly state the ideologies that were part of the conversations? How much did the ways you responded or refused to respond to them inform us of your own ideologies about interculturality? What about your interlocutors?*

**Notes**

1    For an event on interculturality and the COVID-19 crisis that I organised in summer 2020, potential participants were asked to explain why they would want to take part in it. One respondent explained that the topic, which they referred to as 'intertextuality', was of interest to them. There could be an interesting Freudian slip in the use of this other notion.

2 On the Health Care and Well-being page of the University of Helsinki, one section is dedicated to the idea of Culture Shock and its 'stages'. "You might experience what experts call "Culture Shock", a process a person may go through after moving to a different country" (https://studies.helsinki.fi/instructions/article/culture-shock). Needless to say that this ideology has been questioned umpteen times (see e.g. Fitzpatrick, 2017).

3 This refers to the work of the late consultant and social psychologist Geert Hofstede (1928–2020), whose cultural dimensions that he designed for the company IBM in the 1970s have been very popular to deal with interculturality in research, education and the business world. I have reviewed PhD dissertations on e.g. so-called 'migrant-background' pupils, whose interculturality was assessed against Hofstede's work. Needless to say that such studies are ethically problematic since Hofstede's work was designed first and foremost for the corporate world.

4 The writer Zhe Ling (2020: n.p.) comments on this toxic question as follows: "-Where are you from? 4 words. 4. If you are Chinese, you already know that this question is not a good omen. 4, 四 (Sì), 死 (Sǐ), death. It was written in the statement. The question is killing you". (my translation from French).

5 Suddenly in spring and summer 2020, many people seemed to have become 'specialists' of China, Chinese culture, politics and economy, although they had never stepped a foot in the country. Some interculturalists even inserted critical comments about Xinjiang in their publications during the crisis to criticise the Middle Kingdom in relation to democracy and human rights, although: 1. They had very little knowledge about the Uyghur Autonomous Region; 2. Most likely relied on reports from Western media (see e.g. Byram, 2020, footnote 11). While discussing democracy and human rights, these same interculturalists failed to mention (randomly): refugee camps in Turkey, negotiated with the EU; the mistreatment of minorities in different parts of the EU; Antisemitism, Islamophobia and anti-Gypsyism in Europe; police violence and disproportionate use of force against peaceful demonstrators but also the case of Julian Assange in the UK.

6 Robert Musil (1994: 174) defines ideology in an interestingly complementary way: "intellectual ordering of the feelings; an objective connection among them that makes the subjective connection easier".

7 Locally, 'majority' scholars can also play the role of gatekeepers of the kind of knowledge constructed about interculturality that they wish to push for. For example, in a recent event about linguistic diversity, multilingualism and the welfare state in Finland, all the speakers were 'white European scholars' based in Sweden and Finland. Can one talk about this topic, even from a research perspective, when one represents so limited a view of 'diversity'?

8 The Hui people mainly come from Northwestern China and the Zhongyuan region.

# 2   Who was influential in the ways we understand interculturality?

## (A.S.)

I wish to start with these questions: if external objectivity does not exist how do I know if 'my approach' on interculturality is the 'right' one? What if the results from my research articles and even the point of this book may be misconstrued? Does this mean there are no 'rights' or 'wrongs' when researching and teaching about interculturality? These questions were inspired by my reading of Berdyaev (1960: 6) where he wrote: "To know man [sic] in and through man means not to make him into an object. Meaning is revealed to me only when I am in myself, i.e. in the spirit, and when thinghood, external objectivity, does not exist for me. Nothing that is an object for me has meaning". Reflecting on how we see the field, the subjects within our research and teaching, and the differing internal and external worlds of our research require constant criticality. This involves continually questioning my position in research and teaching and that of the other. We are never outside of our research and teaching on interculturality – these constitute acts of co-being and co-experiencing which we share along with other interlocutors (whether that be research participants, colleagues, and/ or the infinite contextual factors and influences).

Questioning our positions in our research also involves probing the realms in which we use certain forms of knowledge and how these processes produce and reproduce different forms of power: in a sense, *dispositifs*[1] that influence and shape how and what we determine as 'knowledge' about interculturality. *Dispositifs* relate to the production and reproduction of power through (security) apparatuses which control and order subjects (see earlier discussions on Althusser in the previous sections). These forces take many guises; they can be technical, administrative, mechanical, symbolic and so forth. Central to the functioning of the *dispositif* is the power-knowledge nexus. The French historian of ideas, Michel Foucault (1926–1984), articulates that,

No knowledge is formed without a system of communication, registration, accumulation, and displacement that is in itself a form of power, linked in its existence and its functioning to other forms of power. No power, on the other hand, is exercised without the extraction, appropriation, distribution, or restraint of a knowledge. At this level there is not knowledge [*connaissance*] on one side and society on the other, or science and the state, but the basic forms of "power-knowledge" ["*pouvoir-savoir*"].

(Foucault, 1997: 17)

For Foucault, the *dispositif* has a productive function that is not the totality of the relationships it gathers under it, but it exists only in relation to the object of its analysis. To put this another way, for Foucault, human beings, and all of the things that constitute who we are, are constituted through the productive forces of the *dispositif*. The Italian philosopher Roberto Esposito (2012) argues that the *dispositif* functions through hierarchising the world. Rather than being equal, these elements are actualised in an ordering [*disposizione*] or more precisely in a *dispositif* that layers or superimposes one under the other (2012: 20). Thus, some regimes of power-knowledge become more dominant than others in the sense that the *dispositif* hierarchises the world.

For Esposito, in *A Thousand Plateaus* (1980), French philosophers Gilles Deleuze (1925–1995) and Felix Guattari (1930–1992) show,

[the] becoming-animal takes on its full constitutive and countering force when we recall that the animalization of man was the most devastating outcome of the *dispositif* of the person, but also of the thanatopolitical powers[2] that imagined they were opposing it while actually enhancing its coercive power.

(Esposito, 2012: 149)

Esposito's critique of Deleuze notes, Becoming-animal is not the darkest pits of our existence nor is it a metaphor or literary phantasm. Rather,

The animal – in the human, of the human – means above all multiplicity, plurality, assemblage with what surrounds us and with what always dwells inside us: We do not become an animal without a fascination for the pack, for multiplicity. A fascination for the outside? Or is the multiplicity that fascinates us already related to a multiplicity dwelling within us? But this also means plurivocity, metamorphosis, contamination – and preventive critique of any claim to hereditary, ethnic, or racial purity.

(Esposito, 2012: 150)

For Foucault and Deleuze the individual has the potential to distance themselves from the *dispositifs* that create our identity. This folding of power
relations opens a space for the individual to transgress. However, it is important to note that this must recognise the agonistic (i.e. combative) function
of power (e.g. Mouffe, 2013). For the Belgian political theorist Chantal
Mouffe this involves not merely how to eliminate power but how to constitute productive forms of agonistic power. The French philosopher and activ-
ist Claude Lefort (1924–2010) sees in conflict the very form of the social,
that is, the social as such is conflictual (Lefort, 2007). If there were no political conflicts, the social would be undifferentiated. It would be a mass made
up of many disconnected individuals lacking a political form (Ibid.). One's
research and teaching about interculturality contains *dispositifs* that function as ideological and political apparatuses. The self, one's work (whether
teaching or research) and the other cannot be separated from *dispositifs*.

These are important considerations in problematising how the power-
knowledge nexus influences 'our' interculturality. Why is it that we are
drawn to certain theories, approaches, methodologies – yet, we reject others? In interculturality one needs to think about the ways *dispositifs* in international academia/higher education can shape and control how and what
we research and teach about. If one thinks about the quotation from Nikolai
Berdyaev (who himself did not write about *dispositifs*) at the start of this
section, deconstructing *dispositifs* is not exclusively orientation towards a
particular strand of research or teaching, an approach or methodology. It
might include some of these things – but ultimately, it involves questioning perceived truths, norms and knowledge. Unfolding dominant *dispositifs*
about interculturality should be about questioning the very essence of things
(subjects, objects and relations). This movement includes problematising
one own's being through the self-other relationship.

My work on interculturality has been influenced by scholarship from Russian literature (e.g. Fyodor Dostoyevsky, 1821–1881), philosophy and literary theory (e.g. Mikhail Bakhtin 1895–1975) and linguistics (e.g. Valentin
Voloshinov 1895–1936) to political theory (e.g. Chantal Mouffe). Yet, perhaps listing my sources of inspiration might, or might not, be so interesting
or important to the reader. But there is an important line in Bakhtin's (2012)
work, "*I live in a world of others words*". This means that the notions/ideas/
approaches that we may think are 'mine' or 'ours', on the contrary, could
not be further from the truth – these notions, ideas, approaches are never our
own. Bakhtin uses the notion of *Raznorechie* (Разноречие) or what has been
referend to as 'heteroglossia' (from Greek *heteros* 'other' + Greek *glōssa*
'tongue, language'; Bakhtin, 2012; Bakhtin, 1984; 1981) in Bakhtin's
English-language translations to refer to the co-existence of a multiplicity
of various struggling language-forms – e.g. social registers, professional

discourses and so forth – associated with certain ideological points of view. This means that all the words we speak, hear, write or think about have been produced and co-constructed through dialogical interactions between the self and others. These movements also involve interactions with systems and structures from macro, meso and micro levels of social interaction – in a sense, all of the interactions between the self and others which co-construct our co-being and co-existence with other human beings. This is why meanings are co-constructed through dialogical relations – between the self and others. Therefore, meaning in itself cannot be reduced down to one person or object. Instead, all of the meanings contained within a given sign leave a trace from our previous dialogical interactions and experiences (e.g. from our interpersonal relationships with friends and family members, our social outlook and worldviews and our education systems to the ways we experience events and situations) – and predict the dialogical interactions and experiences to come because our words are always oriented towards an other, and towards others, when we speak, listen or read the word. Yet, the trace from our previous interactions remains within one's internal comprehension when one actions these words.

Here it is important to question why is it I see this particular notion/idea/ concept/ approach *this* way? How have my experiences and interactions shaped how I see and use these aspects of my work? In a sense, how has the authorship of my work been constructed?

In his work on Bakhtin's literary analyses on the author and hero, Ilya Kilger (2008) argues that Bakhtin shows how the author converts the hero from the category of self to that of the other and thus finds 'herself in a position of remembering the hero after his death, a metaphor resonant with Walter Benjamin's [1892–1940] famous claim that "what draws the reader closer to the novel is the hope of warming his shivering life with a death he reads about"' (Kilger, 2008: 559). Kilger goes on to articulate,

> while the hero-for-himself leads a shivering life, where meaning is always unstable and becoming is constantly becoming, the author, by reproducing the hero's life as fate and flame that consumes it as the flame of meaningful necessity, gives us access, albeit a highly mediated one, to the experience of wholeness and stable being.
>
> (Ibid.)

Although the quotation is about literary theory, it raises a problematique for all authors, including scholars of interculturality, that 'my' work might be used by others to satisfy a particular wholeness or being for another. To put this another way, as authors, are we *really* aware of how our work is used by readers to construct a sense of being or belonging? This could be in the guise of reproducing particular norms, feelings, societal discourses, dominant ideologies and so forth. Yet, Bakhtin reminds us as authors our work is always oriented towards the other and is always co-constructed with others. Thus, as the author cannot have full assurance, knowledge or guarantee from these relationships with the other, the author suffers from *a crisis of authorship* as, the author-hero relationship, like the self-other relationship cannot maintain a stable distance. The author's position is thus "shaken and is no longer considered essential: one contests the authors right to be situated outside lives life and to consummate it" (Bakhtin, 1990: 203). For scholarship and teaching on interculturality regarding the instable distance between self-other, there are important questions here: To what extent do we as authors become consumed in, and by, the ideologies of our work? Or, to what extent as authors do we become consumed by the subjects in our work? Failing to problematise these questions may result in the self speaking *over* or *for* the other. In these processes, the self can violate the other and itself.

In scholarship and teaching about interculturality, always, the definitions, concepts and approaches found within our research and teaching about the notion have been shaped and conditioned by the functioning of differing political and ideological apparatuses. The ways our work are cited and referenced by others also reproduce our own ideological prints on the work of others. Valentin Volosinov reminds us "wherever a sign is present, ideology is present, too" (Volosinov, 1973: 10). Uncriticality towards the concepts, ideas, methods and notions found within the version of interculturality one uses can be problematic. Without critically deconstructing the genealogy and archaeology (linguistically, socially and politically) of the concepts, ideas, methods and notions one uses one can reproduce methodological nationalism (concentrating on representatives of one country rather than looking at experiences with people from other countries), essentialisms (reducing the self and/or other to a singular narrative/essence), stereotypes (generalised beliefs and/or representations), symbolic violence (a form of power whereby one group becomes dominated, excluded, prejudiced against by another – symbolic violence functions through naturalising or universalising power relations through commonsensical ways of thinking and speaking), and prejudice (biases towards a person based on their perceived individual and/or group membership).

The task, whether teaching or researching about interculturality, is always to trace back our steps in questioning why is it that I believe in *x*, why do I choose to use *a* in my work rather than *b* or *c*, or is my take on *y* and *z* correct. These aspects need to be continually problematised in our teaching and research on interculturality. Interculturality, and the notions, concepts and ideas contained within the notion, are polysemic – these multiple meanings may mean one cannot find solace (what Bakhtin calls wholeness and stable being) in interculturality. Thus, our task is always to ask why. If one cannot find solace in interculturality, why not? Or, if solace can never be found in the notion, then to what extent do I impose a version of solace onto others (e.g. through the discourses, ideologies, definitions I use in my research and/or teaching)? As I have noted earlier, *postupok* is a reflexive movement for both the self and others because the etymology of the word designates 'the step one has taken' (past tense) – we have already taken acts which predetermine where we are, in this sense – the words, ideologies, notions contained in 'our' authored works or teaching materials, so our task is to retrace our steps through *postupok*. It is only through engaging in the dialogical relationality between self and other involved in *postupok* that one can begin to understand one's being and the fluctuating positions one takes within one's own work.

**(F.D.)**

*The intellectual*, Edward Said (1996) argues in his 1993 Reith Lectures, must maintain a vigilant skepticism towards the doxa, the obvious and the commonsensical. Interacting and engaging with others, either directly or through what they have written, is the only way to: 1. Identify what is considered 'too obvious' to be true, *the taken for granted*, 2. Highlight and dig into different ideologies and 3. To question all these, position oneself in relation to them and find new ways to forge ahead. This genuine lifelong 'dialogical' endeavour should be systematically reflected in one's work on interculturality.

Paul Valéry (1958: 58) puts it nicely when he writes: "There is no theory that is not a fragment, carefully prepared, of some autobiography". Like all intellectuals, my past, present and future ways of reflecting on, critiquing and proposing interculturality are based on the thousands of encounters that I have had in my life (I was 45 years old at the time of writing). Some of these encounters were meaningless in the sense that they did not transform me[3] (or maybe they did but I did not notice or don't remember why and how); some I have sub/consciously erased from my memory because they were painful, violent, betrayals, etc.; others (re-)shaped me as much as they (maybe) (re-)shaped others. In my private life,[4] many of my close friends and family have obviously had an influence on the way I see interculturality today. Professionally,[5] in summer 2020, I see at least eight people who have helped me to *un-re-think* my ideas about interculturality, most of them have either become good/best friends or people I consider to be family members. These include (the list follows a chronological order in terms of when we met):

• I consider **Marie-José Barbot** to be my academic and life mentor. We have known each other for over 20 years. As a scholar and intellectual, she pushed me to be curious, to read and to be systematically critical and reflexive. She specialises in critical approaches to autonomy in education and was Professor at the University of Lille (France). Marie-José and I organised what I consider to be a very important interdisciplinary event about intercultural encounters in education in Paris at the Conservatoire National des Arts et Métiers (CNAM) in 2011. Amongst the speakers we had Martine A.-Pretceille (education), Michel Agier (sociology), Saksia Cousin (anthropology), and Denys Cuche (cultural studies). The special journal issue we published in French (Barbot & Dervin, 2011), following the event, allowed me to identify further problems with the way the notion of interculturality was used in education (and in the way I had been discussing it in my earlier work). I also started wondering about the difference between interculturality and the way Marie-José problematised autonomy as something that was based on *multifaceted dialogues between self-other* rather than on *self only* – both sounded very similar concepts in a sense (Ibid.).

• With **Anne Lavanchy** and **Anahy Gajardo** we co-edited two volumes on the *Politics of Interculturality* in 2013 and 2014 (one in English: Dervin et al. [2013] and one in French: Lavanchy et al. [2014]). We met at a conference in Switzerland and decided to work on the volumes to untangle further the notion of interculturality – being all dissatisfied with the way it was dealt with in research and especially its depoliticisation. Anne and Anahy are both anthropologists, and I was very excited to start working with people from outside the field of education. The start was a bit of a shock for all of us since we had misconceptions about the notion – or more precisely, about how we perceived each other to understand the notion. For them, as anthropologists, the notion of interculturality was difficult to understand and to use, since *everything was intercultural to them*. They felt that scholars in education misused the term and emptied it of any interesting and challenging aspects – I tended to agree with them although I knew that anthropology was not always immune to some of the critiques they addressed to interculturality in education. The books we co-edited were important milestones for me. I started looking at the notion from an even broader perspective, learning with Anne and Anahy how to unpack it and be critical of our former engagement with interculturality. The issues of translation, etymology/genealogy and knowledge production in different languages and in different parts of the world (they introduced me to research on *interculturalidad* from South America) started to be of interest to me then. My engagement with anthropology, a field I consider to be central, with philosophy, in thinking about interculturality, was reinforced by these book projects. More about anthropology later.

- **Régis Machart** (1968–2016) was the most generous, hardworking and critical scholar I have ever met. For several years, we worked hard to try to make a difference in the field. Like me, he had been 'horrified' by the scholarship about interculturality, especially in applied linguistics. Régis was based at a Malaysian University, where he noticed the damage that an overly Eurocentric form of intercultural knowledge had on local scholars – but also its local politicisation. They rehearsed ideologies from the 'usual suspects', without realising how contradictory they were to the very 'politics of interculturality' in Malaysia. Régis and I organised many events in both Malaysia and Finland, edited several books (amongst others: Dervin & Machart, 2015; Dervin & Machart, 2017; Machart et al., 2016) and set up a book series with Springer (*Encounters between East and West*), as well as the *International Journal of Bias, Identity and Diversities in Education* in 2015. Not a day passed without us talking online, challenging each other. I learnt a lot through our discussions and became increasingly confident that the field had to change (as much as I should constantly reconsider my own perspectives), considering the lack of interculturality in the scholarship that dominated. When Régis passed away in 2016, it took two years before I could start writing again. I missed his encouragements, his friendship and his challenging me. I wrote this tribute a few weeks after his death: www.igi-global.com/pdf.aspx?tid%3D169961%26ptid%3D158823%26ctid%3D15%26t%3DPreface.
- My encounter with **Etta Kralovec** from the University of Arizona (US) is somewhat of a miracle. She had contacted me by e-mail to request a meeting during a 'pedagogical tour of Finland'. Like thousands of other scholars, educators and decision makers from around the world, she had been interested in the imagined 'miracle of Finnish education'. Although I rarely reply to such requests (I used to get hundreds), I invited Etta to one of my research group meetings. We clicked. I discovered someone who had a long and exceptional experience, who was generous, hyperactive, and who had a genuine interest in changing education. We visited each other many times and cooperated on several projects. My visits to border schools in Arizona, where many Mexican children study, crossing the border every day, were fascinating and gave me new research ideas. These visits also confirmed that so-called American multicultural education ideologies were as problematic as 'European intercultural education' and urged me to look for alternatives elsewhere.
- The co-author of this book, **Ashley Simpson**, used to be my doctoral student many years ago. He contacted me from Russia where he was working before his PhD. When I met Ashley, I was impressed. He was extremely

knowledgeable, critical and reflexive and we had one important thing in common: an interest in M. Bakhtin's dialogism. Ashley and I have written extensively on the European ideologies of interculturality and on the political manipulation of discourses of democracy and human rights.[6] One day at a seminar, a colleague who was listening to Ashley told me that we two were so similar: sharp, straight to the point and . . . critical. We have organised many events together, taken part in EU-sponsored projects. Like the other influential colleagues and friends, Ashley has (re-)introduced me to many interesting voices that have enriched my way of thinking about interculturality (e.g. Chantal Mouffe's work on democracy, certain aspects of M. Bakhtin's work of which I was unaware). Co-writing this book is another opportunity for me to move forward with my work on interculturality, since our dialogues are always enriching and fruitful.

• Since 2018, I have been fortunate enough to be a visiting professor in intercultural studies at Karlstad University (Sweden). My cooperation with **Andreas Jacobsson** there has also been stimulating. Andreas and I have organised many events (amongst which an international conference on interculturality in teacher education), co-written articles and are currently finalising a book on interculturality in teacher education and training (Dervin & Jacobsson, 2020). Andreas is originally from the field of film studies and, like my other influential figures, he is dissatisfied with the way interculturality is dealt with in education, especially with the overly Eurocentric orientation. His curiosity and criticality have also pushed me to un- and rethink my way of problematising interculturality and to identify contradictions and/or potentially Eurocentric modernist ideologies.

• I met **Mei Yuan** from Minzu University of China (Beijing) three years ago. We have been cooperating for two years, collecting data, debating and discussing, and writing articles and books. Mei and I are already very close friends who do not hesitate to be openly critical towards each other. We share the same kind of humour. Through Mei, I have learnt to decentre even more from the limited ideologies that are present in me. When we started cooperating, we decided that we would force each other not to accept our ideologies without questioning them and that we needed to take the idea of 'co-constructing' new knowledge seriously. Mei is the first Chinese scholar with whom I have been able to develop this kind of relationship. I think that this has to do with the fact that, together with our colleague Sude, Mei specialises in Minzu education (so-called Chinese ethnic minority education). Their approach is different from other Chinese scholars who specialise in intercultural communication education, which is too much dominated by the 'West'. So, in a sense, they haven't been 'brainwashed' and 'ordered' to think about interculturality by the big figures of the field such as Byram, Deardorff or Kramsch (who dominate the Chinese field of interculturality). My acquaintance with the field of Minzu, our joint research in Inner Mongolia, Qinghai (Chinese province spread across the high-altitude Tibetan Plateau) and the campus of Minzu University of China have opened up my eyes to the real problems that we face when we try to deal with the notion of interculturality: 1. We use the same words and phrases when we talk about it in English, but we do not necessarily mean the same thing or connote them the same way. Mei and I systematically have discussions around words in English and Chinese and try to renegotiate what they mean to the both of us. 2. There are other ways of thinking about diversity[7] in education and we must 'unearth', listen to these other voices and learn from them. Currently, Mei and I are writing a book about such voices, having interviewed different scholars and students of Minzu, with an aim to enrich current discussions of *diversity education*. I feel very fortunate to have the opportunity to work with Mei Yuan and her team. My love for China (which is no secret) is reinforced by Mei's (critical) friendship and vital intellectual inputs.

This brief introduction to eight scholars who have had an influence on my work does not probably do justice to their full contributions and to the complexity of our cooperative acts (e.g. disagreements, misunderstandings, arguments, unbalanced power relations). What is more, through these scholars, I have been able to meet people whom I do not mention here, but who also most likely had an impact on the way(s) I see (and not see) interculturality. However, I feel it was important for me to introduce them a bit so that our readers can see that a scholar's work is never individual but based on a complex (and sometimes inconsistent) long-term network of influences – to which I cannot do full justice in a few paragraphs. I believe that this 'exercise' (reflecting on other people's influences on us) is an important one to become aware of how one has changed in relation to interculturality ideologically. When I say *change*, I do not mean in some sort of a straight line, but in inconsistent and incoherent ways, going back and forth between intercultural ideologies.

After reading my contribution to this chapter, Ashley sent me these very important questions, which I reproduce here – and which link up to his text above:

Are the people aware of the positions you have given them (friend/best friend/colleague etc.)? Were the positions negotiated? How? How did you deal with imbalanced power relations (e.g. doctoral student and doctoral supervisor/mentor and mentee)?

How do you ensure that these people are not merely a confirmation of, or reflection of, your worldviews and your work?

These are indeed very relevant questions, which we should all consider when running through the archaeology of our thoughts about interculturality. To make it fair, it should also be done with others so that one can contrast impressions of ideological, economic-political influences, co-learning and relations (during and after cooperation).

Although I limited this brief presentation to scholars, it is also important to reflect on other individuals who have shaped our ways of thinking about interculturality (from a cashier in a store who might have triggered a new idea to a family member who has made us rethink our views). Interculturality, like other human phenomena, can only be approached through other people's input. In that sense, interculturality as a notion is 'alterophile'. To go back to Valery's quote from the beginning of this section, our autobiography does play an important role in this process of *un-re-thinking* interculturality and should not be silenced.

Now I would like to discuss the intellectuals and scholars who have also influenced me through their writings. Let me start with a cliché: Reading should be the basis to developing critical thinking and reflexivity. Reading should help us dig deeper into interculturality and to critique it, rather than just worship what is said about it. However, I believe that it is rarely the case when I review papers about it. People will mention Byram and Deardorff for example without engaging critically with their 'ideas'. Engaging with someone's ideas is not just about treating them like mere information or worshipping them and thinking like these scholars and intellectuals, but to un-re-think with and through them. For the French philosopher Bernard Stiegler (2015), global capitalism and the economic ideologies that go with it prevent us from struggling against *systemic stupidity*. The philosopher argues, for example, that "having totally abandoned the task of making Europe a scholarly society, the European Commission has committed itself exclusively to constituting the European market and to submitting academic life solely to efficient causality, thereby confusing knowledge and information" (2015: 218).[8] Often, the literature on interculturality is treated as mere information that one cannot or even should not question.

The Romanian philosopher and essayist Emil Cioran (1911–1995) asserts that, "A book should open old wounds, even inflict new ones. A book should be a danger" (1985: 45). Most of the scholars that I am going to mention below have done just this to me – and thus urged me to move forward in my attempt to re-un-think interculturality. I have also come to reject many of the ideologies that their writings have 'imposed' onto me.

In a recent e-mail interview, a scholar asked me *who my role model in intercultural communication* was. Surprised by the idea of having a role model, I responded:

> I have no role model either in 'intercultural communication' or in 'intercultural education'. My inspiration comes from my long-term engagement with sociology (e.g. sociology of postmodernity), philosophy (e.g. process philosophy), linguistic discourse analysis (e.g. enunciation) and social psychology (e.g. dialogism), amongst others. Many thinkers have been important in shaping and reshaping my thinking about interculturality, but I don't consider any of them as 'role models'. As an intellectual, I believe that role models are dangerous, especially if they are worshipped in a way that makes us blind towards scientific incoherence and political manipulation. We need to be independent and critical thinkers to move forward, not followers of any guru or scientific tribe. I believe that there are too many 'Western' gurus in the broad field of intercultural communication education (Bennett, Byram, Deardorff, Kramsch, etc.) and that their input needs to be systematically questioned. Such role models kill the diversity that intercultural research should work on.

When I met my PhD supervisor for the first time, she told me that the research plan I had sent her beforehand was "boring, uninteresting and repeating the same as everybody else". She then asked me to "read everything" and to come back with a new research plan when I was ready. My original research plan was about 'assessing international students' intercultural competence in Finnish higher education'. I knew it was not good. I knew that it was just rehearsing what everybody else had said about the topic. I knew it contained the doxa of the time about the slippery concept of *intercultural competence*. I knew that what I was proposing was contributing to the neoliberal ideology of interculturality as a *mere competence*, a mere call for 'adapting', 'adjusting' and 'behaving' rather than thinking and questioning (Stiegler, 2019).

What I did not realise, though, was that the scholars to whom I referred in the plan were only either the 'classics' of interculturality (E.T. Hall and even Hofstede) or British and French scholars from applied linguistics and language education who had dealt with the issues from mere 'communicative' and 'cultural' perspectives (e.g. Byram, Zarate), and that these were insufficient in the sense that what they were saying about interculturality was either extremely old-fashioned (e.g. in the way they used the concept of *culture* in comparison to anthropologists of the time) or unreflexively 'Western'. What the research plan contained was some sort of mythology about interculturality that I was proposing to spread even further.

From that moment, I endeavoured to 'read everything' I could put my hands on, regardless of the field of research. I took a year off to read scholars from linguistics, sociology, philosophy, social psychology, anthropology, cultural studies, etc. Some authors I had read before, but I wished to rediscover. After a year of exploration, I started to realise that, regardless of disciplinary boundaries, there were more similarities than differences in the way scholars discussed issues of e.g. identity, representation, group or diversity. This was also very useful to explore the archeology of the concepts, notions, theories and methods that are used in the field of interculturality. The need for real interdisciplinarity (navigating meaningfully and coherently between fields without even noticing) became my way of approaching research on interculturality. I then moved away from *nissology* (a reference to the study of islands on their own terms) in intercultural scholarship. The Chinese philosopher Zhuangzi (2013: 136) summarises well this endeavour:

井蛙不可以語於海者，拘於虛也；夏蟲不可以語於冰者，篤於時也；曲士不可以語於道者，束於教也。今爾出於崖涘，觀於大海，乃知爾醜，爾將可與語大理矣。

A frog in a well cannot discuss the ocean, because he is limited by the size of his well. A summer insect cannot discuss ice, because it knows only its own season. A narrow-minded scholar cannot discuss the Tao, because he is constrained by his teachings. Now you have come out of your banks and seen the Great Ocean. You now know your own inferiority, so it is now possible to discuss great principles with you.

But we need to be careful about not getting lost in the *Great Ocean*. In a recent article about arts in languages and intercultural citizenship education that I have received, I realised that the authors were navigating from one scholar to another (or one institution to another), while composing an ideologically problematic patchwork of ideologies. The article starts with a quote by J. F. Kennedy and alternates references to (in alphabetical order) Appadurai, Byram, Camus, Dewey, Kramsch, Harper Lee, Saramango, as well as full references to the UNESCO and the Council of Europe. In an e-mail to a list about intercultural communication education, a student from western Asia was asking for help in combining Brazilian philosopher and educator Paolo Freire's[9] ideas about critical pedagogy and a famous British scholar of intercultural competence – whose ideologies are in direct contradiction to the former. These patchworks would deserve to untangle the opposing ideologies of these different voices – often found under the surface of what they write and say.

My own work on interculturality has been based on a 'lucid menagerie of voices', with very few voices from intercultural communication education being included (currently, probably none), not because I wish to silence them but because I often feel that the arguments, the theories that are proposed are to be found elsewhere, often in a different era (e.g. discussions around mobility, essentialism and culturalism). I thus prefer to go back to the roots of the problem and to acquaint myself with the scholars from other fields of research who have looked into these issues at first. I often 'hurt' when I read e.g. an article which attributes a concept or an idea to an interculturalist when they were enunciated well before in another field. 'My' interdisciplinarity has caused a few problems. For example, some colleagues consider my work to be 'outside the field' – since I don't mention their work. This has been the case with a few journals, for example a US-based journal asked me to add references to papers published in the field of intercultural communication, especially those from the journal (I retracted my paper). Some colleagues have also called my work "very philosophical", which has always made me laugh. I assume that very few philosophers would see my work as a serious piece of philosophy.

Two further points before I present the publications that have had an influence on my work:

- I always tell my PhD students: "*If you can read in any other language than English, please do, and include these references in your work*". I have reviewed too many articles, book proposals and PhDs that are monolingually written in English, even if the scholar can read in other languages. Navigating knowledge through different languages can help to see interculturality from different perspectives, to reflect on translation and ideologies (Cassin, 2016). It is thus vital to do it. However, ideas and works in other languages should not just be used as 'mere decorations' but help build up alternative ideologies about interculturality, and thus be included at the centre of argumentation.

- After the aforementioned year that I spent "reading everything", whenever I would start reading a new book on my interests of the time (mobility, migration, identity), I found that I had reached a stage of *saturation*, i.e. although the writers might have been using different terms to label the realities they were discussing, the core of the argument tended to be the same. This is where fiction – which I had neglected – came to the rescue. For the French philosopher Jacques Bouveresse (2008), the border between philosophy and literature is not always clear. I would tend to argue the same about research on interculturality. For example, I have found the book *A concise Chinese-English dictionary for lovers*, published by British writer Xiaolu Guo in 2008, to be inspirational to reflect on identity, language and the issue of race. The same applies to a novel by Chinese writer Lao She (1899–1966) entitled *Mr Ma and Son* (2014). In this book, Lao She tells the story of a Chinese father and his son relocating to London in the early 20th century. I have read this novel many times, and I always find it very relevant for reflecting further on 'East-West' perceptions. I re-read *Mr Ma and Son* a few days ago and was surprised (again) by how similar discourses on the Chinese are still today. This is what Lao She says about the way Brits saw the Chinese back in the 1910s: "Chinese transformed into the most sinister, most foul, most loathsome and most degraded two-legged beasts on earth. In this twentieth century, people are judged according to their nation" (2014: 34). There are many other novelists who have influenced me and that I have referred to in my work.

If I look at my research output over the past 20 years, I can see clearly how my interests in specific topics/individuals related to interculturality have been guided by my reading and, at the same time, by encounters and trips (in a somewhat chronological order):

- (European) modernity and postmodernity and their impact on ideologies
- Strangeness, mobility and migration
- Identity/identification vs. culture
- Dialogism
- Epigenetics (the study of changes in gene expression)
- Henri Bergson's Process Philosophy
- Nation branding and education export (marketing the [imagined] attributes to sell)
- Critiques of 'Western' social justice, human rights and democracy
- Confucianism/imagined China
- Minzu education.

A somewhat quick and limiting overview of my readings over the years could be summarised as follows. This provides our readers with insights into my intellectual navigations, while presenting them with some reading that I find to be central in re-un-thinking interculturality:

1   Globalisation is not a new phenomenon and discourses about interculturality as something reserved to the 21st century are inaccurate (I often note that many publications in the field start with the cliché that *the world has never been as global as it is today*; an assertion that should be revised). Pieterse's (2004) *Globalization and Culture: Global Mélange* as well as Goody's (2006) *The Theft of History* have provided excellent food for thought by showing that globalisation has always been with us and that the West has manipulated histories to make it look better and more important from a Western perspective than other parts of

the world (see e.g. Goody's [2006] fascinating discussions about how the West invented the idea that the concept of love is a Western concept). Sanjay Subrahmanyam's (2011) *Three Ways to be Alien* examines the story of three figures (e.g. a 'Persian' prince at Goa in India) whose 'floating' identities support the need for critical global history in rethinking today's world. These arguments are further developed by Valerie Hansen's (2020) *The Year 1000: When Explorers Connected the World—and Globalization Began*. She discusses, for example, the presence of blonde-haired people in Maya temple murals at Chichén Itzá (Mexico), which might indicate the presence of Vikings.

2  I then started reviewing critically how the concept of identity had been used in research on interculturality, especially in relation to the idea of culture. The following books remain very important to me – although I have become more realistic about their implications: sociologist Zygmunt Bauman's (2004) *Identity*; sociologist Michel Maffesoli's (2000) *The Time of the Tribes*; economist Sen's (2007) *Identity and Violence* (which I discovered in Mumbai), psychologist R.D. Laing's (1969) *The Divided Self: An Existential Study in Sanity and Madness* as well as political scientist Bayart's (2005) *The Illusion of Cultural Identity*. While I was reading these books, I also reread philosopher Henri Bergson's work, which is often labelled as Process Philosophy. His book (1911) *Laughter: An Essay on the Meaning of the Comic* was a revelation to me. In the book, Bergson demonstrates convincingly that laughter keeps our minds and social engagements elastic beyond the solid outlook that they can take on. What all these scholars asserted was that identity is not a pre-given (although it often appears to be in administrative terms and when treating each other like identity controllers), and that it is something that people co-construct with others in specific contexts and times. They also allowed me to identify many preconceived ideas that were circulating in the field of interculturality: the 'false' dichotomy of *individualism vs. collectivism*, the ideology of *culture shock* disguising politico-economic issues, etc. While I was reading about identity, I 'dug into' the critiques of the concept of culture, especially around the tough debates that anthropologists had in the 1980s. I always felt that this concept was given too much importance – and I did not understand it. As a young PhD student, I remember asking a 'guru' of interculturality at an international conference (they were treated as such) what they meant when they said *culture* (a word that they had used repeatedly in their keynote), to which they replied, "it is too complicated to define it". Many of their followers agreed with them on that day, showing the danger of tribal prejudices. The ideas of *culture as an excuse*[10] and *culture as something that is changing* made me rethink what interculturality was about. Norwegian anthropologists

Unni Wikan (2002) and T. H. Eriksen (2001) helped me to sharpen my critiques of the concept. The same goes with Swedish anthropologist Ulf Hannerz (1996) and Joana Breidenbach and Pál Nyíri (2005).

Before moving on to the next 'archeological point', I would like to take a short break to insist on the importance of the field of anthropology on my un-re-thinking interculturality. Many anthropologists have opened my eyes to what I considered to be problems in the field of interculturality. Amongst others: Gerd Baumann's (1986) *Contesting Cultures*; French anthropologists Alban Bensa's 'human-sized anthropology' (2010) and Eric Chauvier's 'anthropology of the ordinary' (2017). In 2008, I co-organised an international conference in Paris, France, entitled *Anthropology, Interculturality and Language Learning-Teaching: How compatible are they?* Having noted the omnipresence of some form of anthropology/ethnography (the two words were usually used interchangeably) in the field of interculturality – *anthropology of the distant other, anthropology of the near, anthropology of mobilities and intercultural encounters, cyberanthropology, auto-ethnography* – the purpose of the conference was to examine the miscellaneous ways of using such a complex discipline as anthropology and its methods in language learning and teaching and to gather some of the leading specialists interested in these methods. Thomas Hyland Eriksen was one of the keynote speakers. In his closing paper, he noted that the kind of anthropology that we were doing in the field of interculturality was "a remnant of the history of anthropology" (*à la* Levi-Strauss) and that no real anthropologist would label what was presented as anthropology *anthropology*. What the conference made me realise was that: 1. We must dig properly into the archeology of ideas and methods before 'robbing' them; 2. Interdisciplinarity cannot work if we don't scrutinise the changes occurring in other fields.

3    Although it became clear to me that identity, culture and togetherness were changeable and malleable, I was dissatisfied with the way they were 'proved' to be in analytical terms. Many scholars would make the claim that they are 'liquid' or 'fluid' but dealt with them as if they were solid or as if they could be solidified. I have read or heard many scholars say: "identities are changeable, never static" and then say and even write things such as "but Italians do this or that". This is where my background in linguistics was relevant. Having been trained as a linguistic discourse analyst, especially by French linguists, it became obvious that the little-known French enunciation theory for the study of speech and thought presentation could be central in proposing an interesting way to bridge the gap between the contradictions of 'liquid' and 'solid' ways of conceptualising interculturality and to show the

co-construction of such discourses, without attempting to find some 'Truth' about who people are. This theory was inspired by the work of Bakhtin, Jakobson and Benveniste (amongst others) and looks at language in relation to users and contexts. Kerbrat-Orecchioni's (2014) work on enunciation, Ducrot's (2018) split subject, Paveau's (2006) theory of pre-discourse are good starting points and have been presented in English by Marnette (2005) and Angermuller (2014). Dialogism and polyphony (or the idea that any discourse is a response to previous discourses, and thus enters into dialogue with multiple and often unidentifiable voices) have also had a major influence on my work, and often go hand in hand with postmodern conceptualisations of identity and togetherness (e.g. Roulet, 1991). In 2008 (Cambridge) and 2010 (Athens), I took part in the interdisciplinary international conference on the dialogical self and discovered that many scholars from around the world were looking into similar issues as I did, using dialogism inspired by Mead and Bakhtin. Through the work of Ivana Marková, Per Linell, Michèle Grossen and Anne Salazar Orvig (2005), I was introduced to the method of focus groups to explore socially shared knowledge. British social psychologist Alex Gillespie's (2006) book *Becoming Other*, which also relied on dialogism, inspired me and is very relevant for the field of interculturality since he looks at the positionings of Western tourists in India.

4    After years of struggles to try to propose something different in relation to interculturality, and especially after my colleague and friend Régis Machart passed away, I felt somewhat 'stuck'. I had nothing else to say, nothing new to propose. The field seemed to be moving in a different direction but, unfortunately, I felt that the alternative ideologies that I had contributed to develop were becoming somewhat clichés ('liquid identity', the word 'interculturality' became mainstream but misunderstood). China saved me from this and, to borrow a metaphor from the German mathematician and natural philosopher Gottfried Wilhelm Leibniz (1646–1716) about the exchanges he had hoped for between Europe and China, "a Commerce of Light" started between the Middle Kingdom and myself (Perkins, 2004). Since I was able to make yearly trips to do research there, I started to see new issues that needed to be explored. I read a lot about how China had been imagined and 'culturalised' by the West since the 18th century. French sinologist Anne Cheng's lectures at Collège de France (and her introduction to the intellectual thought of China, 2014) helped me to get a good understanding of the issue. Through her, I was able to reread critically Confucius's *Analects* and to understand that I had completely misunderstood what was said in the book (which he did not write since it is based

on 'transcriptions' from his followers). In 2012 I had already written an article where I had looked at how white English-speaking scholars had misused some form of Confucianism to examine the experiences of Chinese students in the West. I spent two years reading different translations and commentaries on the *Analects*. I realised that the *Analects* could well serve as an excellent textbook for interculturality since the ethics that it presents (which is NOT about conformism, acritical filial piety, etc., see Dervin, 2020), can help us rethink how to address encounters from modest but firm, reflexive and critical perspectives. Actually, as Nelson (2020: 14) notes, the term *Confucianism* (a term invented by Catholic missionaries in late Ming and early Qing dynasty) refers to "the rich and varied traditions of reflection and argumentation in premodern and modern China, Korea, Japan, and Vietnam" called *East Asian ruist (rujia 儒家) philosophies*. It is not a unitary system of thought that can be summarised by clear-cut characteristics, but it focuses on what could be considered important aspects of interculturality: *socially oriented personal self-cultivation and learning and self-reflection*. For Nelson (2020: 18): "Thinking mutates, spreads, and transverses multiple divergent discourses in which unique configurations of interpretation and contestation unfold. Confucius and Confucianism are interpretive discursive formations formed through imaginative projections and constructions and through encounters and communicative interactions". This had rendered Confucianism to me a plural and multifaceted ethics that needs exploring again and again. During my stays in China, I have also come across the writings of Swiss Sinologist Billetier,[11] whose approach to translation of Chinese philosophy has had an influence on my work; Barthes's (2013) book about his travels to China; and I rediscovered the work of Marxist philosopher Louis Althusser. Becoming familiar with Chinese writers such as Lu Xun (1881–1936) allowed me to look at the issues of identity and interculturality from a more creative perspective. Finally, through my involvement with scholars of Minzu ('Chinese minority') education, I have acquainted myself with research on this form of education. I have found most research published in English on the topic to be problematic. Written by Western scholars, Chinese scholars based in the West, or by Western and Chinese scholars from the Mainland, the papers and books published in English tend to follow Western canons of research methods and theoretical frameworks and to start from negative entry points (injustice, discrimination, etc.). Sude and Yuan's writings (e.g. Yuan et al., 2019) have helped me to get a sense of the achievements of diversity education in China while pointing at some of more realistic issues. This has helped me to see that, when it comes to interculturality, Western education faces in fact very similar problems as China, and while the Chinese have seemed eager to find inspiration from us for these issues, I argue that we need to learn from China. My work with Yuan and her team is a contribution to triggering interest in Minzu (Yuan et al., 2020; Sude et al., 2020).

*This is the second time in my career that I take the time to look back and to reflect on what I have experienced in relation to scholarship on interculturality. It has now become clear to the readers, I suppose, that very little of what I (claim to) think about interculturality comes from me. Like all scholars, in a sense, I am like an airport, a system of nods and networks, welcoming many and varied people who pass through or stop while rejecting some (!).*

## Notes

1  French word for *apparatus, device, unit, appliance* and even *machine.*
2  Which relate to the politics of and over death.
3  Are encounters meant to 'transform' us?
4  On further consideration, the division between *the private* and *the professional* appears utterly artificial. However, I wanted to focus here on people who have contributed 'in the open' to my work, by e.g. publishing with me. The reader can refer back to my publications to 'witness': 1. The influences these scholars have had on my way of reflecting on interculturality and 2. The changes and potential contradictions they have triggered in my work diachronically.
5  Had I been involved directly in politics or in 'fraternal organisations', I would also have spent time here listing their influences.
6  In an online petition against China back in Sept. 2020, a Nordic individual wrote in a very arrogant 'saviour-like' manner: "Because I work with China in research and education and somehow would like to coach in my little way the country towards more inclusion".
7  On the thorny concept of diversity, see Hinrichsen et al. (2020).
8  Looking at the many EU projects and networks on interculturality through which people are made to develop a pre-determined set of competencies – embedded in the ideology of the European identity – and to play games to learn, one can see the confusion between knowledge and information noted by Stiegler.
9  (1921–1997).
10  A good example of culture as an excuse is to be found here: "A British person: I can tell you must be a Chinese from the way you speak English. You speak English with a Chinese accent". This is followed by (Chinese cultural characteristics) as a way of explaining the Brit's assertion. Actually, this is about language rather than the 'stop gap' of culture here.
11  See *Interpreting China for the West* – Jean François Billeter (n.d.) for an introduction to his ideas in English. Retrieved September 18, 2020, from www.youtube.com/watch?v=cthAXVJuu_Y.

# 3 How does intercultural research and education influence experiences of interculturality?

(A.S.)

What is meant by experience in interculturality? Scholarship and teaching on interculturality are seemingly obsessed with representations about experiences – e.g. the experiences of migrants living or working in different spaces and places, experiences of international students studying abroad, the experiences of newcomers to new locations and so on. Yet, to what extent does this represent a narcissistic self-congratulatory immersion in the experiences of the other and otherness? Could this actually be code for the imposition that the other needs to conform to some ideological or prescribed ideal in order to 'be' or 'become' more intercultural (whatever this may or may not mean)? The ways in which people are categorised and labelled in research on the intercultural ('the migrant', 'the refugee', 'the newcomer') represent biases of how the people behind the labels and categories are represented. It can be limited and limiting to view people this way as people become 'boxed in' by static representations. In these instances, seeing people exclusively as an other, through their otherness, negates the dialogues necessary to move beyond surface appearances and representations. If difference in interculturality is only what you want to see, then difference is all you will see.

For the Hungarian Marxist philosopher and literary critic György Lukács (1885–1971), "Any gesture with which such a man might wish to express something of his experience would falsify that experience, unless it ironically emphasised its own inadequacy and thus cancelled itself out" (Lukács, 2010: 23). This provokes the reader to problematise how we understand our experiences – what we might think is a particular form or type of experience, others and the other might think otherwise.

Lukács argues that people cannot translate an experience to an outward act, feeling or behaviour – that is because experiences are internal manifestations. These internal manifestations can only be understood through engaging with the self and other. The quotation from Lukács demands another implication for one to think about. If one's understanding about one's experiences is inadequate (we orientate internal subjectivities to distant objects), then one needs to think about how the signs and representations about our experiences are constructed. In a sense, how do we attribute meaning to our experiences?

In interculturality, one needs to ask the following questions about our experiences: To what extent are encounters or experiences about interculturality simulated? To put this another way, to what extent have the acts already been predetermined and decided for us (how both the self and the other will act, behave, gesture, speak)? And, to what extent are our experiences about interculturality mimicked or copied in order to satisfy the demands of our self and/or that of the other?

In order to problematise one's experiences about interculturality, one first needs to think about how one gives meaning to experiences through the signs, images and representations one uses. On images and representations, the philosopher Gilles Deleuze argues "the copy is an image endowed with resemblance, the simulacrum is an image without resemblance" (Deleuze, 1990: 257). This means, the copy or simulation is an image with resemblance (by definition, the copy resembles the thing copied), whereas the simulacrum is an image without resemblance (e.g. man is made in the image of God, according to catechism, but since the fall – i.e. because of his sin – he no longer resembles Him). Deleuze goes on to articulate that "simulation is the phantom itself, that is, the effect of the functioning of the simulacrum as machinery – a Dionysian machine. It involves the false as power" (Deleuze, 1990: 263). Thus, the simulacrum is not just a degraded copy, Deleuze argues, it has its own positive power, which interrupts the relation between original and copy. His example of this is pop art, which in his view pushed the copy so far it became a simulacrum, an image without resemblance (e.g. American artist Andy Warhol's famous Campbell's Soup prints) (see Deleuze, 1990: 263; Deleuze, 1995: 294).

Often in interculturality, our experiences and interactions are marked by the simulacrum. The simulacrum is not the same as the previous image because it contains the likeness, and importantly, the difference of the differentiated image. In interculturality, our experiences are based upon how we perceive our self, or that of the other. We make judgements or acts based on how one thinks one is being perceived by the other, or by what one perceives the other is demanding from them. This happens at a particular time within a given contextual situation. We know from the previous sections of this book, though, that this distance between self-other can never be stably maintained. Here, instead of falling into the trap of reproducing previous intercultural encounters or simulations, the image that is actually reproduced is similar and different than the original image. In this sense, the image of the simulacrum functions as a superimposition over the original image.

Examples of the simulacrum functioning include the simulacrum of 'The Black Man' being a criminal. The simulacrum of 'The Black Man' has a long history of discursive association with vice and violence. The Black Lives Matter movement, a vehicle for articulating the systemic disenfranchisement of Black people globally, has been read by many in the media and by some leaders as an expression of 'thug violence'. Here, the colonial image of 'The Black Man' as being 'savage' and 'barbaric' is now superimposed by the 'Black Man as criminal' image today. The reproduction and likeness of the colonial images, and the representations attached to the discourses, are maintained through the positive power attached to the differentiated copied image. This superimposed simulacrum now functions as an omnipresent image.

Another example of a functioning simulacrum is a phenomenon which has swept across many contexts over the past couple of decades, what the French philosopher Étienne Balibar calls "racism without race" (Balibar, 2005). Here, the original image of race is a biological construct whereby some races are deemed as being inferior to others (e.g. the supremacy of some races over others). The original image of race as a biological construct is displaced by the renewed images and representations of 'culture' and of 'cultural differences' towards the other. Anne Phillips argues that the displacement of 'culture' for 'race' focuses on "the harmfulness of abolishing frontiers, the incompatibility of life-styles and traditions. That the discourse employs the language of culture rather than race does not ensure its innocence" (Phillips, 2009: 56). In this instance, the phantom of prophylaxis or segregation (the need to purify the social body, to preserve 'one's own' or 'our' identity) functions as simulacrum. The simulacrum superimposes the copied image of 'culture' and 'cultural differences' over the image of 'race', whilst the remnants of the original (biological) image of race still remain attached to the sign.

Deleuze goes on to argue that the oneiric (related to dreams and dreaming) function of the simulacrum means, "it renders the mind attentive and makes it choose the most suitable phantasm from among all the subtle phantasms in which we are immersed" (Deleuze, 1990: 276). When given the choice in these experiences, the self often returns back to how it perceives the most suitable phantasms – often from those that have already been preconfigured beforehand through one's experiences and interactions.

With this in mind, I often feel Deleuze's reference to the oneiric function of the simulacrum relates to both the fields of intercultural education and intercultural communication whereby researchers and teachers are often made to "choose the most suitable phantasm from among all the subtle phantasms in which we are immersed" (Ibid.). I would like to take this opportunity to propose a popular phantasm that researchers and teachers of the intercultural often use: *the simulacrum of the liberal interculturalist*. The liberal interculturalist simulacrum contains the image that the self needs to be compassionate, tolerant and respectful of the 'other's culture'.

Like our previous discussion on the simulacrum of racism without race – whereby, representations about race are displaced by images of culture and cultural differences, I argue the liberal interculturalist image falls within this same mantra. Calls for the self to be 'more intercultural' vis-à-vis the other reproduces a symbolic violence towards the other (a form of power whereby one group becomes dominated, excluded and prejudiced against by another – symbolic violence functions through naturalising or universalising power relations through commonsensical ways of thinking and speaking). The original image here is not the same as the image in the race without race simulacrum (i.e. the biological image of race) – but of the superimposed simulacra of culture and cultural difference. Here, the self produces and constructs its own mediated (simulacra) dialogues with the other which become the main takeaway image and representation, rather than that of 'meaningful' and 'authentic' dialogues with the other. This is what Deleuze calls the doubled condition of the simulacrum. Deleuze gives the example of people who have faith in God to illustrate this point,

Hence the believer does not lead his life only as a tragic sinner in so far as he is deprived of the condition, but as comedian and clown, a simulacrum of himself in so far as he is doubled in the condition. Two believers cannot observe each other without laughing. Grace excludes no less when it is given than when it is lacking.

(Deleuze 1995: 95)

The image of the self being compassionate, tolerant and respectful becomes the omnipresent representation for how people *are* and how they *ought* to be. In such instances, the self can pretend to simulate dialogues with the other to mimic or copy this image for affect (we have no way of knowing if this is their sincere or real intention to be respectful, tolerant, etc.) whereby the self becomes seduced by the image of its own likeness and grandiose. In this sense, the liberal interculturalist simulacra becomes a self-indulged phantasm *par excellence*. In this instance, the simulacrum superimposes the copied images of 'compassion', 'tolerance' and 'respect' over and through the images of 'culture' and 'cultural differences'. The omnipresent image which remains is that of the self being compassionate, respectful and tolerant, whilst the representations of culture and cultural difference still remain attached to the sign.

When thinking about a personal experience about the simulacrum and about my work on interculturality, an instance when I first moved to Finland to start my PhD came to mind. In one of the first few days of living in the country, I went to a shopping mall near to where I was staying, and I went to a telecommunications store with the aim of getting a mobile phone contract. I entered the store and asked one of the customer service representatives about my query. Because I had only entered the country a few days earlier, I did not have a Finnish social security number so I could not get a mobile phone contract at this instance. The customer service representative replied by saying "because you are a foreigner, we do not know whether you are going to pay your bills on time, so you need a Finnish social security number. Have a nice day". In this instance, the simulacrum of the foreigner reproduces representations of the other as being 'strange', 'different' and 'barbaric' – someone 'who cannot be trusted'. Here, the image of the foreigner being strange and untrustworthy is engendered through representations about the state (e.g. the reference to the Finnish social security number, which guarantees [or gives the illusion of guaranteeing] safety and trust in a sense). These representations reproduce an 'us' versus 'them' logic, whereby foreigners cannot be trusted, contra to 'Finns' who can be trusted (something which you often hear about Finland and its people, especially in the field of education). Like the example of 'The Black Man' earlier, in this instance too, the simulacrum of the foreigner is that of someone who is potentially a criminal who will break the law (e.g. the reference to not paying bills). The simulacrum functions through creating an image that Finns can be trusted (the preservation 'one's own' or 'our' identity). This image is superimposed onto and through the image that 'foreignness' should be viewed with scepticism and suspicion. The omnipresent image which remains is that of 'Finns' being trustworthy.

When one thinks about one's experiences of interculturality, one needs to question how and why these experiences have been shaped and formed by particular simulacra, "in any case, simulacra are everywhere. We do not cease to be immersed in them, and to be battered by them as to be battered by waves" (Deleuze, 1990: 275). If the functioning of the simulacrum means that the constant repetition of images, discourses and signs are a false infinite (false impressions of will and desire), then it is important for critical interculturality to develop counter narratives allowing us to escape from specific dogmas and impositions through proposing counter-images and counter-practices – again and again. The time has come to denounce and de-myth false phantasms that have produced false images about the purpose and aims of teaching and researching about intercultural education and intercultural communication over the past few decades. Only when one has moved away from and denounced the gods and phantasms of *the simulacrum of the liberal interculturalist*, can one move towards critical interculturality.

**(F.D.)**

I always find it hard to believe when a colleague asserts that their research did not influence their lives (or vice versa). I have heard this argument many times from people who work on interculturality and who claim objectivity in the way they deal with interculturality. But how can they separate what is happening in their office and classroom and in the outside world?

In what follows, I discuss how my engagement with interculturality as an educational and research object has shaped my own experiences of interculturality. I am limiting my discussion to three points that I consider to be essential when I think about my own experiences of interculturality: 1. *I lived by the slogans of the moment*, 2. *Identifying/playing/rejecting power games*, 3. *Fighting against Finland hysteria in education.*

## *1   I lived by the slogans of the moment*

When I started working on interculturality in my mid-20s, I used to be confused about who I was (being urged and forced constantly to put my identities on the table), about the questions that I kept trying to answer (the sempiternal "where are you (really) from?", "what is your mother tongue?", "in what language do you dream?", "what is your nationality?", "is your name Irish?" – questions I still hear again and again today but mostly ignore) and about the unsatisfactory way(s) research and education were trying to prepare people for interculturality. There were times when I even avoided being in situations where I would meet someone for fear of having to hear these questions again and to be forced to provide a single answer (and thus a single story). For Sartre (1964: 364), "I am possessed by the Other; the Other's look fashions my body in its nakedness, causes it to be born, sculptures it, produces it as it is, sees it as I shall never see it. The Other holds a secret – the secret of what I am". What the philosopher means here is not that the Other 'knows' me, but by their very presence, their gaze, they 'possess' a piece of me, which may or may not be who I feel is me. There were other times where I felt ashamed of not being able to answer these questions, ashamed of not being able to play the game that others seemed to be playing happily. The worst moments were when people 'ordered' me to be what they fantasised I was for them. Over the years, I developed a certain number of strategies to deal with these 'police inquiries'. Depending on my mood, my (often wrong) feelings about my interlocutors, their reactivity or the potential intertextuality between us (someone reminding me of someone else, impressions of déjà vu, etc.), I would:

- Play the game and perform a single identity (limited to one passport), a bit like Caulfield in Salinger's *The Catcher in the Rye* (1958: 87): "I am

always saying "Glad to've met you" to somebody I'm not at all glad I met. If you want to stay alive, you have to say that stuff, though".
- Ignore the questions and either try to shift the discussion in another direction explicitly or implicitly or escape from the situation.
- Perform a fake identity since any discourse on a given national identity will systematically lead to imagining our interlocutors.
- Joke about the question and offer a surrealist answer.
- At times, I got upset and angry about having to answer these questions again.

Increasingly, we hear of many people recounting having gone through the same painful 'police inquiries'. Some international students I had 'shadowed' for weeks in Turku (Finland) were increasingly tired of being asked the question of origins all the time, again and again, especially by the same people. Italian students I interviewed many years ago explained how they had started performing being Italian the way some Finnish students had fantasised them to please them (being late, hugging all the time, etc.). In a 2017 event, American actress Uzoamaka Nwanneka Aduba explained how she wanted to change her first name because "no one could say my name". When she told her mother to call her Zoe, she replied: "If they can learn to say Tchaikovsky and Michelangelo and Dostoevsky, then they can learn to say Uzoamaka" (www.colorlines.com, 2014).

For Mantel (2008: n.p.), "to be born at a certain time is to live by the slogans of the moment, to take your place in the giant skipping game with its formalized chant". The slogans of *national culture*, *identity* and *community* (amongst others) always hide behind these problems. When I started forming a sense of interculturality beyond the accepted forms of the time (essentialism and culturalism, with a communicative twist), I realised that the way we were dealing with interculturality was based on remnants of another era (European Modernity). The frustrations and contradictions that I have experienced (MY complexities and other people's versus the 'order' to simplify ourselves) were based on a historical mistake in a sense (i.e. *who are you?* in the singular).

What I learned through my research and teaching is that we don't have to answer these questions, that we don't have to be governed by others' questions (or govern others with these questions as a matter of fact). As intellectuals and educators, we need to help people who are 'powerless' (e.g. their national or linguistic identity might place them in an inferior position because of societal discrimination) to build up the strength/discourses to answer and/or resist these questions if they wish to move away from the modernist ideology of intercultural encounters. There is not one way to resist but many different ways, and it is important to take contexts and interlocutors into account when deciding how to deal with these issues.

Refusing to answer the question, "Where are you from?" can sometimes lead to conflicts if it is done in an abrupt way. On the other hand, the tone of the question (again like a police inquiry) might trigger emotions in us that we cannot control and, sometimes, it is also important to speak one's mind, especially if one feels uncomfortable. Honesty is also a form of respect for self and the other. Humour can often defuse such situations. There are other ways of engaging with the other, for example: *What is your favourite colour? (referring to a jacket someone is wearing) I have seen a very similar jacket in a store in Japan, what do you like about it? What is your favourite food?* (I am sure that the reader will find more stimulating questions).

If we reject today's slogans (which I believe we should in a sense), we could foster some curiosity in meeting others in different ways. At the same time, we should respect their freedom to keep quiet about their origins, languages and belongings. As if we had an ant's antennae, we need to be sensitive to the questions we ask, not so much to censor what we want to say or ask, but to make sure that others are comfortable *a minima* with answering these questions. If I feel that someone is unwilling to answer a question or appears to be embarrassed, I just let go. Going back to other types of questions we could try to ask, the question of *why do we always introduce each other by mentioning our nationality?* is an interesting one.

## 2   *Identifying/playing/rejecting power games*

Every year, I meet hundreds of people. The older I get, the higher I go in academic hierarchies, the more people I get to meet. When I was a young scholar, I was a mere 'spectator'. Now I have been fortunate enough to have had hundreds of students and audiences listening to me around the world. I always feel embarrassed when people come to me and say, "I am a big fan of your work". I often respond: "And I might be one of yours soon". I have voiced my dislike for 'gurus' and admiring people since they lead to creating boundaries and hierarchies between us. I am not naïve. I know we cannot do away with boundaries. However, as an intellectual, I feel that our duty is to lower them since we have all been 'beginners' and 'spectators'. No one is better than others. We are always beginners of interculturality – because our identities, being and belonging are always in the making. No one can conquer interculturality. Academic status or publications should not rule over the way we 'do' interculturality together.

The person does not exist as such but relies on the presence of at least one other person to do so. Sociality is based on both exterior signs of identification (e.g. skin colour, economic status, age, etc.) and the figment of our imagination of us and them (Maffesoli, 2000). As asserted many times already in our book, no one can escape from the hyphen between them and

others. What my scientific and educational engagement with interculturality has revealed to me is how much power relations, symbols and statuses
govern relationships. Robin Lakoff's (1992) book was important for me to
deepen my understanding of these phenomena. According to Lakoff (1992:
17), our 'collective ego' (Maffesoli, Ibid.), or the unavoidable complex
enmeshments of us and them, "our every interaction is political, whether
we intent it to be or not; everything we do in the course of a day commu-
nicates our relative power, our desire for a particular sort of connection,
our identification of the other as one who needs something from us, or vice
versa. Often, perhaps usually, we are unaware of these choices; we don't
realise that we are playing for high stakes even in the smallest of small
talk" (Ibid.: 17). This is why we all need to 'save face' (not just Asians as
pseudo-theories want us to believe) when we talk to and deal with others.
This is why we lie or silence our thoughts sometimes not to embarrass ourselves or others. And this is why we sometimes manipulate others by making them believe in e.g. the power of 'our' culture and/or language ("you
cannot understand because you don't speak my language").

We need to learn to identify power games in intercultural encounters.
Such games depend on representations of, amongst others, our status as
('native') speaker of a given (powerful/'small') language; our nationality,
origin, skin colour; our gender; signs of economic status. Once we are aware
of these and know how to identify signs, we need to reflect on our actions:
*What are my own 'powers'? What powers seem to be attributed to me? Can
I afford to play these 'power' games or not? What is at stake for my interlocutor and me? If I reject these games, what will be the consequences? How do
I include dealing with emotional reactions in having decided to reject power
games? Should we discuss them with those around us? How do we misuse
certain status indicators such as nationality, culture and language to position each other? Why do we use them and in addition to what other indicators (gender, religion, etc.)? Can we re-balance power relations together?*

Through my research, I have realised that one cannot do away with issues
of power when one examines situations of interculturality.

## 3   *Fighting against Finland hysteria in education*

Most of my academic career has taken place in the Nordic country of Finland (five million inhabitants). A relatively 'young' country (100 years since
its independence from Russia), like most countries around the world, Finland is in the process of redefining its identity within the 'ocean' of globalisation. Before the 2000s, the country was hardly ever mentioned abroad.
4.12.2001 marks an important date for Finland. This is when the results
of the first Programme for International Student Assessment (PISA) of the

OECD were released. Finland came first, which put the small Nordic country on the map for many years and earned her the status of 'educational utopia'. It then seemed that the whole world was interested in the Nordic country. The triennial international survey aims to evaluate education systems worldwide by testing the skills and knowledge in reading, mathematics and science of 15-year-old students. Around 510,000 students from 65 countries participate in the assessment. PISA has managed to establish an increasingly strong and mediatised 'comparative turn' amongst educational systems around the world, where top systems attract attention and become models for others (Grek, 2009). For Finland, this represented an opportunity to 'rebrand' itself through the process of Nation Branding and to attract many 'pedagogical tourists' to the country. The concept of country branding has been introduced by e.g. Melissa Aronczyk (2013) and Simon Anholt (2009). Aronczyk defines country branding as:

> Using the tools, techniques and expertise of commercial branding is believed to help nations articulate a more coherent and cohesive identity, attract foreign capital, and maintain citizen loyalty. In short, the goal of nation branding is to make the nation *matter* in a world where borders and boundaries appear increasingly obsolete.
>
> (2013: 12)

In the document entitled *Mission For Finland* published in 2010, the Finnish authorities place education at the centre of the nation branding strategy. The document also justifies the need for nation branding in the following terms:

> *1) Increasing the appreciation of the fruits of Finnish labor, that is, promoting the export of Finnish products and services, 2) Promoting international investments in Finland, 3) Promoting inbound tourism to Finland, 4) Promoting the international status of the Finnish State, 5) Promoting the appeal of Finland among international professionals, 6) Raising the national self-esteem of Finns.*
>
> (CBR, 2010: 23)

Interestingly, nation branding represents, in a sense, a 'renationalisation' of Finland, a new phase in defining Finnish people's identity and appeal to the world through the forces of the market. Of course, Finland was not the first nation to explicitly brand itself in 2010. As a 'smaller power' in the world, Finland needs to legitimise its very existence and nation branding represents a powerful way to do so, especially as Finland has had a good reputation in most international rankings.

In 2012 I started working at a department of teacher education in the capital city, Helsinki. Before that, I had a position in the humanities in a less influential university. The shift between fields occurred easily as part of my research in the other Finnish university had involved work on language and intercultural education. However, the major difference was related to the considerable implicit emphasis on 'promoting and selling Finnish education' that my new position entailed. I became intrigued by the mantra of 'the best education system in the world', and the visits of hundreds of 'pedagogical tourists' in search of the 'miracle of Finnish education' (Niemi et al., 2016) in my new department. But what was most surprising was the omnipresent use of the expression 'Finnish education export' to which the department contributed actively.

Since the 'PISA hysteria' started in the 2000s, imaginaries about Finnish education have blossomed: *Finland is one of the most equal countries in the world; Finnish people are hard-working and honest; Finnish children do not need to work hard at school even if they perform excellently in PISA studies*, etc. (Dervin, 2013). Decision makers', country branders', practitioners' and even researchers' voices from Finland have contributed to spreading this common sense, supported by international media, politically engaged scholars and foreign politicians in need of inspiration. Critics of PISA have noted many methodological concerns about the conduct, analysis and interpretation of its results (e.g. Goldstein, 2004). For instance, I have been personally very critical of interpretations such as the following, concerning Finnish pupils' excellent results at reading:

> This is due to both educational and socio-cultural reasons: teaching children to read in school is based on individual development and pace rather than standardised instruction and frequent testing; Finnish parents read a lot themselves and also to their children; books and newspapers are easily available through a dense library network; and children watch subtitled TV programmes from early on.
>
> (Sahlberg, 2011: 25)

Although Sahlberg's arguments include larger societal aspects such as TV and reading outside schools, it seems to me that too much emphasis is laid on the positive influence of parents and teachers. I believe that looking into the specificities of the Finnish language, which has regular spelling, compared to e.g. speakers of English, should retain our attention. While in Finnish every single letter is pronounced, English pronunciation is quite challenging as the way words are written rarely correspond to how they are read aloud. Take for example the words *Leicestershire* [ˈlestəʃə(r)] and *Marimekko* in Finnish. Ignoring this aspect can rhetorically serve the purpose of showing the 'superiority' of Finnish education and society (teachers are excellent; parents caring, etc.). I have often felt very uncomfortable with this uncritical claim.

Such imaginaries about Finnish education often construct Finland as a different place that has very little in common with other countries – especially in terms of education (Sahlberg, 2011). The insistence on dissimilarities makes the Nordic country both an 'exotic' place and a 'better' place. Finland has somewhat understood the value of these aspects in advertising and selling its educational system. Adopting an ambiguous form of *bovarysm* (Gaultier, 1902), through which Finland is constructing as better than she is, those who sell implicitly or explicitly its education often lessen the value of others by othering them and representing them as 'bad examples' to follow (the case of China) or as being ruthless and even 'primitive' forms of education. In 2015, I published the chapter *Is the Emperor naked? Experiencing the "PISA hysteria", branding and education export in Finnish academia* (Dervin, 2016). In 2019, my Chinese book entitled *The Best Education in the World? The Myths of Finnish Education* was released in China (Dervin, 2019). In these documents, I discuss how my work on interculturality has allowed me to uncover the strategies used by education exporters, Finnish companies, scholars and educators to sell Finnish education, Finland and imaginaries about Finnishness. I have often tried to tell my interlocutors around the world that the image that they tend to have of Finland is pure imagination, a form of doxa, hidden under the power of the corporate world. For them, I have tried to unveil the aforementioned misrepresentations that they are often fed with. But sometimes I have tried in vain . . . people often remind me that "it is better than in my own country in any case" (including many so-called critical scholars). Ashley and I have also published extensively on the problems of Finnish education export (Simpson, Chen & Dervin, 2019; Dervin & Simpson, 2019).

## [Synopsis]

Chapters 2 and 3 were based on two questions:

* Who was influential in the ways we discuss interculturality?
* How did intercultural research and education influence our own experiences of interculturality?

Although our responses were formulated and presented differently, these are the common points that we both made:

### Educators' and scholars' knowledge of interculturality

* A given educator's and/or scholar's knowledge is always based on a complex network of influences (other scholars, institutions, political affiliations, daily encounters, etc.). There is a need to be aware of such influences *a minima* when engaging with scholars' ideas. This is impor-

tant as it can help us identify 'hidden' elements with which we might otherwise disagree (for example, an affiliation with a fraternal organisation, which might add extra layers of meaning to the way a scholar or an educator discusses interculturality) and try to avoid 'systemic stupidity'.

- Not all scholars have equal access to global platforms to voice their views and share their research about interculturality. The way research and education about interculturality is organised tends to be unequal, with a preference for knowledge produced in English-speaking countries and promoted by influential supranational institutions, publishers and journals.
- All intellectuals face pressure from (global) apparatuses and *dispositifs*. It is thus our duty to: 1. Identify such pressure, 2. Be transparent about, discuss and problematise it and 3. Distance ourselves from knowledge that is overly dependent on these forces.
- A given scholar's work on interculturality witnesses/should witness change in paradigms, use of concepts and notions and methods throughout the years. When engaging with their ideas, we should be aware of these changes and endeavour to consult their latest publications.
- Most knowledge produced about interculturality is said to be interdisciplinary. If so, we must reflect on the benefits and drawbacks of interdisciplinarity, what interdisciplinarity could be about and 'dig' in the archaeology of e.g. a given concept across fields of knowledge.

## The enmeshment of different contexts in the way we discuss interculturality

- One cannot separate contexts of research and teaching of interculturality from other contexts that we scholars and educators cross (home, hobbies, services, etc.). They affect each other, *nolens volens*. We should recognise these constant mutual influences, by speaking and writing openly about them.
- A scholar's and/or an educator's economic-political and ideological views and life experiences do influence their take on interculturality, even when (and especially) they claim 'objectivity'.
- We need to be aware of the fact that the enmeshment of these different (sometimes conflicting) contexts may lead to simulacra of interculturality to 'muddy the water'.
- Working on interculturality can open our eyes to other 'bigger' societal phenomena, which may seem unrelated at first (e.g. the dominance of corporate power in education).

**Remaining critical and reflexive at all times**

- There is a danger of worshipping certain 'role models' in the field of interculturality, especially if they come from privileged and hegemonic contexts. We should reflect on, problematise and question their ideologies and positions. Their ideas cannot just be treated as mere information about interculturality.

- Working on interculturality in research and education requires being vigilant and sceptical towards what is presented as the 'obvious' and the 'commonsensical' (e.g. in the choice of a word, in a set objective for intercultural learning).

**[Going further]**

Readers might want to consider asking themselves or others the following questions to continue reflecting on how they understand interculturality:

- Are you aware of who might have influenced the way you think about interculturality? Any scholar? Any acquaintance?

- How would you respond to the question: "Do you have a role model in the field of intercultural communication education?" If you happen to have a role model in the field, what do you know about them? For example, about their political beliefs and affiliations, the economic forces that support their work, etc.

- Take one concept or notion that you find essential in reflecting on interculturality: How do you define it? Why do you define it this way? Who might have influenced you? Do you know other ways of defining it in your language and other languages?

- Where does your knowledge about interculturality as a notion come from? Geopolitically, where would you situate the theories, concepts and notions that you know?

- When discussing interculturality, have you found yourself in a situation where you realised that your interlocutor and yourself did not share the same understanding of what it is about? How did you react? Were you able to negotiate a basic understanding? Why do you think you did not share the same discourses on the notion?

- Do you 'practice' interdisciplinarity? What are your principles?

- Has your way of understanding interculturality changed since you started engaging with the notion? Can you do an archeology of your engagement with it? Think about an influential scholar of interculturality, can you do the same with their ideas?

- As someone involved in researching or teaching interculturality, what would you say your responsibilities are in front of your students?

# 4 Can we prepare/get prepared for interculturality?

**(F.D.)**

*Problematising 'preparation'*

*Preparing for interculturality* often relates to teaching, educating and/or training in somewhat formal contexts. But *preparing for interculturality* also includes, in a sense, daily reflections on how we behave with and think about meeting the other. The verb *to prepare* comes from Latin *praeparare*, "make ready beforehand". Asking if one can prepare or get prepared for interculturality is asking if one can be 'made ready before' one experiences it, which, most likely, will materialise in the encounter of (at least) another person. Does it make sense? If interculturality is a 'never-ending' process of renegotiations, thinking, unthinking and rethinking, and bearing in mind that every single individual whom we meet is unique, while sharing similarities and differences with us, can one (be) prepare(d) for it? Meeting different kinds of others in/formally, face-to-face and/or in a mediated way (online, through a book, a film, etc.) is what social beings do throughout their lives. Is there thus a need to prepare them? *Would we teach, educate and/train people to breathe? To eat and drink? To have sex?*

From birth, we (are) systematically prepared/prepare to meet others – many different kinds of other people – often without realising.

We reflect on encounters all the time since the Other's voice is always part of us – and vice versa.

We create scenarii in our heads: *Am I going to feel comfortable with this particular person? What are we going to talk about? Is s/he lying to me? Why do I feel s/he is in love with me? I hope s/he does not look at me straight in the eyes.*

We re-/play encounters in our heads before, during and after we meet others (and so do they!). These encounters also contain intertextual references that bring us back to previous (or future) encounters: *a fragrance, a place, an accent or a facial expression* transport us to a potentially complex network of past, present and future encounters.

We have been trained and educated to meet people in certain ways – often depending on how we perceive their gender, age, social status and the potential benefits we can get from them: How we greet them, how to be 'polite'[1] to them, how to formulate our thoughts in ways that include them. In some cases, we have been asked/trained to smile – or not, to shake hands – or not, to hug – or not, to keep eye contact – or not, etc.

*Many of my friends note that I have an automatic smile when I am in a shop. "A fake smile" they call it. A smile I put on without even realising when I wish to thank someone. In most cases, I don't even think I mean to smile. I know this comes from my parents, who did the same. I just copied them, and like an automat, I reproduce their smile when I meet someone in a shop.*

Sometimes we 'lead' encounters, sometimes we are 'led' by the Other. Sometimes we feel comfortable, sometimes we don't. Sometimes we want encounters to end quickly, sometimes we want them to last. Some encounters are purely transactional, others are more personal. Some encounters lead us to flirt, to 'want more', others repulse or anger us. Some encounters are easier than others – automatic, robot-like: *on the phone with a sales assistant, sometimes with family members.* There is not much to lose, as if we were guided by a GPS. Other encounters can represent high stakes and our heart starts beating.

*We learn by meeting. It works well. We make mistakes – big/small ones. We agree, we disagree, we are unsure. We move on.*

How do we then prepare for all these diverse situations and case scenarii? Can there be a one-size-fits-all method to meet others – even if they come from a different 'country' (if that's interculturality!) and speak a different language?

Let's now consider several aspects of encounters that force me to answer in the negative to these questions.

Meeting someone is performing. Being surrounded by people always leads to a performance, willy nilly. Everyone performs. That's why we can never be sure that the other will perceive and experience the encounter we co-perform the same way as we do (*satisfactory, pleasant, horrible . . .*). In *Being and Nothingness* (1964: 59), the French philosopher Jean-Paul Sartre (1905–1980) gives the example of a waiter he observes in a café:

> His movement is quick and forward, a little too precise, a little too rapid. He comes toward the patrons with a step a little too quick. He bends forward a little too eagerly; his voice, his eyes express an interest a little too solicitous for the order of the customer. Finally there he returns, trying to imitate in his walk the inflexible stiffness of some kind

of automaton while carrying his tray with the recklessness of a tight-rope-walker by putting it in a perpetually unstable, perpetually broken equilibrium which he perpetually reestablishes by a light movement of the arm and hand. All his behavior seems to us a game.

In many situations, we behave like Sartre's waiter. We use mechanisms (e.g. 'my' smile, questions such as 'where are you from?') and we perform who we think we are, who the other is or who the establishment, the doxa wants us to see in us and them (*the waiter plays at being a waiter in a café*). Sartre (1964: 60) adds: "(the waiter) plays with his condition in order to realize it". Maybe we also believe that by playing our 'intercultural' conditions we realise interculturality. However, I argue that we only realise the conditions, not the realities.

The French philosopher Denis Diderot (1713–1784) has proposed the idea of the *paradox of the actor* in a dramatic essay of the same name (1773). In the essay Diderot explains that great actors don't experience the emotions they are displaying but are simply guided by their intelligence to 'perform' them. When we meet other people and are prepared to, I believe that we face this paradox: we often lack authenticity (if there is such a thing!), we become *an Other to our otherness*, we play to be: a professor, a man, a European citizen, and at times a Finn, a Brit, a Chinese, etc. Since we have been told through education and commonsense that, in e.g. intercultural situations, we need to show empathy to others, be curious about their culture and demonstrate tolerance, we are tempted to 'play' the one who does all this. But we then meet the Other as *an Other* ourselves, not as someone who is ready – willing? – to build a relation that relies on the *inter-* of interculturality, whereby we could try to renegotiate who we are with and for the other, and be more flexible and less 'guided', or maybe less 'made ready beforehand' (*praeparare*) for something that one cannot prepare for – interculturality.

Since we have no choice but perform who we think we are/should be/are asked to be (*the one I encounter and myself*), it is difficult to know what level of performance we are having. And thus, it is hard to prepare for – and not recommended? – encounters.

Another issue that we cannot do away with when we meet another person is that of the potentiality of *misunderstanding* – and maybe *non-understanding*. British philosopher K. Popper (1902–1994) puts it nicely when he suggests (2002: 29): "Always remember that it is impossible to speak in such a way that you cannot be misunderstood: there will always be some who misunderstand you". Words are never as transparent as we imagine them to be. They get distorted, misused, misplaced and, often, out of our control. Speaking 'perfectly' in a given language does not guarantee 'real' dialogue either.

Misunderstanding differs from non-understanding in that the latter refers to a lack of possible dialogue since (one) of the interlocutor(s) do(es) not comprehend what the other is saying and non-understanding to an illusion of understanding based on false interpretation, experienced by (at least) one of the interlocutors. In many cases, interlocutors who are aware of these phenomena may not even mention them to the other, not to create tension, to 'respect' the other . . . to perform. They might then pretend to dialogue. Mis- and non-understanding are part and parcel of our *modus operandi* and are not always identifiable. Thus, preparing to 'avoid' or 'negotiate' these two essential components of human communication is, I believe, illusionary. If they can be spotted, revealed and/or (re)negotiated, they could lead to interesting discussions and, maybe, to a 'miniscule' step closer to dialogue. However, I do not believe that there are 'techniques' that can be learnt to avoid or 'heal' them.

Our tendency to treat the other as a mere object also represents a major obstacle to preparing for interculturality. We always meet the other through the prism of images, *imaginaries*, that we create of ourselves and them, of contexts and situations, times, experiences. . . . In other words, we don't meet them, but images of them. *We get to see them from afar . . . as much as they get to see us from a distance too.*

For the French writer André Malraux (1901–1976), "The human mind invents its Puss-in-Boots and its coaches that change into pumpkins at midnight" (1967: 23). Preparation to 'avoid' these fantasies, through e.g. work on stereotyping and representation, is often meaningless since one cannot get rid of these elements. Think about stereotypes. We might be aware that they do not make sense, and yet, they remain within us, they emerge when we are confused and do not know how to react in a given situation – or they get replaced by other stereotypes. The other behaves in a certain way (most likely in reaction to our own behaviours or to something we said), we do not understand why and we need to look for explanations in some kind of fund of 'knowledge'. *Everybody does it.* No one is immune against these phenomena:

> Old Françoise has the common idea as regards the English – that they are mad, and liable to do the most unaccountable things at any moment.
> (Christie, 1923: 22)

> The British "knew all about Chinamen", one well-informed young traveler to China in the 1920s pronounced: "They were cruel, wicked people".
> (referring to an article distributed around the Home Office in London in the 1920s, Lao She, 1929: 5)

These assertions on people are there because we need them to believe that we can make sense of this world, of those who compose it. Knowing the other, who they are, is impossible – as much as knowing ourselves, since we need this mysterious Other to make sense potentially of who we are. To quote Malraux again (1967: 23), Man (sic) is "a miserable little pile of secrets". We thus need stereotypes and representations to rationalise them. We need them to reassure ourselves in front of the mystery that the other represents. We need the illusion that we have met them before we actually meet them. Stereotypes are obviously painful. Unlike many educators and/ or scholars whom I have met, I don't believe that it is fair to say that some stereotypes are 'good', 'positive'. Stereotyping is about power relations; it is about inequality. Even if it is formulated in a way that could appear positive to someone, through the in/direct comparison that a stereotype contains, someone always gets considered negatively. For instance, the other day, I overheard a White Finn saying to an Asian-looking person: "I know many people from your country; you people are super nice". I don't need to comment on the emptiness of such a statement (which some might see as 'interculturally positive', others 'interculturally correct') but what it says indirectly is that some other people are not 'super nice'.

One question that I consider important in these discussions is that of the boundary between what is considered as 'knowledge' about a 'culture', a 'people' and e.g. stereotypes about them? To the question "what do the Chinese think about the West?", the French sinologist Anne Cheng (2016) maintained, in a somewhat irritated manner that

> everybody knows here that the Chinese population has now gone over one billion count . . . and I also hope that people remember that the Chinese territory represents by itself practically a whole continent, this is why I cannot reply honestly to this question.
>
> (our translation)

Had she answered by sharing a pseudo-Chinese 'opinion' (or even two or three), these would have passed as stereotypes rather than 'knowledge' about a people. Knowledge about the other often overestimates their uniqueness (Goody, 2006) and boxes them in categories that often contribute to flatter the ego of the one who utters it, in the sense that such knowledge requires comparing at least two entities. Comparison cannot but lead to limiting and judging and in most cases, hierarchising.

The role of education in 'preparing' us to 'do' interculturality needs to be discussed at this stage. Education cannot but be ideological and political. It forces us to believe in certain ideas that are passed down onto us by supranational institutions (e.g. the OECD, the EU in my part of the world) and presented to us as unquestionable. In relation to interculturality, education is 'indoctrinating' us to believe that the way it suggests we meet the Other is *a good way* – see the only way. It thus presents us with magic methods and tricks, half disguised under slogans such as 'we must be tolerant', 'we must respect other cultures', 'we must avoid culture shock', etc. Education also tries to 'programme' us for encounters. In a recent textbook on intercultural encounters mentioned at the beginning of this book, *Experiencing global intercultural communication: Preparing for a community of shared future for mankind and global citizenship* (2019), the authors often present intercultural preparation as programming, focusing on stereotypical pseudo-theories such as individualism vs. collectivism,[2] high context vs. low context, spatial zones according to nationality, etc. – making statements such as "Chinese do not directly disagree because they do not want to appear impolite", without questioning such obvious generalisations and the ideologies hidden behind each word ("disagree"? "directly"? "impolite"?). The authors even use some pseudo psychological 'methods' to prepare the students: "reflect upon your personality", "describe, reflect and critically evaluate different types of personality", etc.

Intercultural 'gurus' are used to support educational goals (im-/explicitly) – gurus whose work is sponsored by neo-liberal, white-dominated supranational institutions and by the corporate world (of academia). The use of these gurus should be questioned in education. As such, educators and students should be made aware of their background and ideologies – I have already said it many times in this book.

Let me discuss two examples here: The case of Hofstede, whose work is often used in education, is interesting. On the businessman's website about his 'cultural dimensions' (labelled as Geert Hofstede[TM]), the following quote appears: "Culture is more often a source of conflict than of synergy. Cultural differences are a nuisance at best and often a disaster". If culture is a problem, then we need to invest in ourselves to make sure we eradicate this problem. Another interesting case is how the concept of *intercultural dialogue*, an omnipresent concept in education, is defined on Wikipedia. Noticing that the concept does not have an entry in the online encyclopedia in summer 2020, an American scholar decided to write it. A quote from Leeds-Hurwitz (2014, n. p.) opens the definition with what I consider to be another negative ideological bias: "Intercultural Dialogue occurs when members of different cultural groups, who hold conflicting opinions and assumptions, speak to one another in acknowledgment of those differences". Interculturality here again is about 'difference', 'groups', 'conflicts'. The references used in the entry to support a definition of intercultural dialogue are mostly from the 'West' (except Nazan Haydari) and seem to be related to the US-based Center for Intercultural Dialogue (CID). Interestingly, the entry makes a reference to an article that I co-published in 2012 (Riitaoja & Dervin, 2012). The quote from this publication in the Wikipedia entry asks questions which, in the way intercultural dialogue is constructed in the entry, were somewhat ignored:

> Who is going to learn about whom, and whose knowledge is to be learnt?
> Does the other have an opportunity to be seen and heard as a subject or relegated to a subaltern position?
> Are knowledge and understanding about her constructed with her and in her own terms?
> Will a religious 'subaltern' ever be equal to the majority in schools?

The way we name things (*Intercultural Dialogue*) always reflects limited knowledge, and relegation of the Other to inferior positions. Writing a Wikipedia entry is a way of influencing how the world sees itself too.

So, the way education projects interculturality always derives from how supranational institutions spell out interculturality, in cooperation with 'gurus' who 'sell' them models of global, intercultural and transcultural . . . competence. In Europe, for example, this often translates in education telling the 'guest' (e.g. so-called migrants) how they should meet and adapt to the majority, behave like them, think like them (often through concepts that I consider to be euphemisms such as 'culturally responsive', 'inclusion', 'adaptation', etc.) – in other words, their minds and behaviours should be domesticated, leaving behind thoughts and behaviours that 'we' consider to be 'primitive', 'closed' or maybe even 'savage'. At the same time, decision makers might tell them that they respect their culture, followed by educators, scholars and students who are made to learn about 'cultural difference'. In the end, the guest's culture is relegated to 'folklore', wall decorations and stereotypes. The 'guest' must start believing in 'our' democracy and human rights – because 'we' assume they know nothing about them. We even monitor some of them against religious radicalisation in e.g. Europe. *The 'guest' must then mimic 'us' politically while we learn about their culture to 'welcome' them. As long as they are 'transformed' politically, façade interculturality can start – but they need to become 'us'.*

Rarely does education suggest a form of interculturality whereby people are entitled to re-negotiate together the basis of their encounters and their dialogues, which are programmed to happen in certain prescribed ways. They are 'ordered' to think about them in these ways – other ways being considered intolerable or insupportable. For instance, while reviewing a European project about interculturality, I realised that the teachers involved in the project were disappointed that their students discussed what they called 'banal' things such as rap music, series on Netflix and did not seem to be interested in discussing about their (national) cultural differences. The teachers had 'tacked' their own fantasies on what interculturality should mean for the students . . . judging their behaviours based on these fantasies. This is exactly what ideology is about. As Roucek puts it (1944: 480):

"Ideology" means strictly a system of ideas elaborated in the light of certain conceptions of what "ought to be." It designates a theory of social life which approaches the facts from the point of view of an ideal, and interprets them, consciously or unconsciously, to prove the correctness of its analysis and to justify that ideal.

By ordering us to think about intercultural relations and encounters in (often) limiting and limited ways, Kant's *Mündigkeit* (*maturity, majority, responsibility*) or our ability to use our reason without being led by another, gives way to our inability to use our own understanding without the guidance of another. For the French philosopher B. Steigler (1952–2020) "the liquidation of maturity (is) based on the reign of stupidity and of cowardice and viciousness" (2015: 3).

Interestingly, research on the preparation of students for interculturality hardly ever examines how students perceive and criticise the ideologies passed onto them in intercultural communication education but focuses on how they are able to 'parrot' – or not, rehearse – or not them. They also get judged for not being able to fulfill these 'invisible' orders (from "they still have many stereotypes" to "they are able to deal with this topic from a democratic perspective" – which make no sense).

Beyond this indoctrination, education for interculturality also often serves as 'self-help' psychological guides to the students to give them the impression that interculturality is something that should be experienced nicely and problem-free: "now I am able to control culture shock", "now I know that stereotypes are bad and must be avoided", etc. In a study about some Chinese students' learning experiences of intercultural communication education at a university in Shanghai, I noted with Hui (Hui & Dervin, forth.) that the students used such 'self-help' discourses when they were asked to discuss what interculturality was about after the course ("I realised that I was experiencing culture shock", "I need to develop this savoir-être",etc.), while they used more personal, 'open' and ideologically different elements when they discussed concrete intercultural encounters that they had had ("we were all young people who shared similar fears for the future"). When they referred to the course, the students also 'parroted' such ideologies as "we must be careful not to make intercultural mistakes", "we must not create culture shock and threaten other people's face interculturally", "we must tolerate their behaviours", etc. These become placebos for a real world that is not always (and should not be considered to be!) *nice*. The saying

甘蔗没有两头甜 in Chinese, which translates as, "You can't expect both ends of a sugar cane are as sweet", is a reminder that, like all social experiences, interculturality should not be treated as a *Disneylandified* context of encounters, where everything looks happy, sweet, respectful, easy, comfortable and conflict-free. The realities of the real world represent concrete contradictions to these ideologies.

I realise that I have opened many doors in my contribution to this chapter. Figure 4.1 summarises the gist of my arguments:

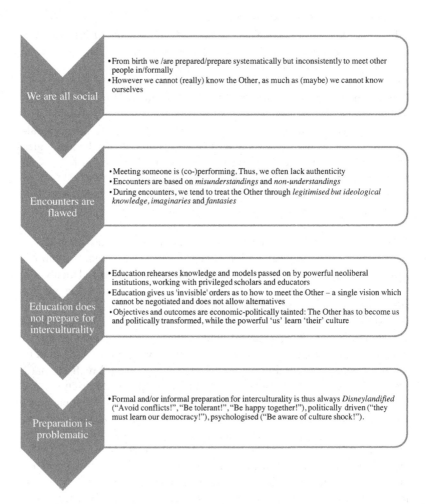

*Figure 4.1* Some 'advice' to prepare to be unprepared for interculturality

So, after all this, preparation appears to be a weak option for interculturality. In this section I am trying to reflect on how to unthink acts of preparation that are put forward for us, so we could *prepare to be unprepared* for encounters.

Let us start with an important comment from the French semiotician Roland Barthes (1915–1980). In his account of his 1974 trip to China, Barthes is disappointed at the ways his travel companions and the 'Westerners' he meets in the Middle Kingdom tend to treat China solely in what he describes as two opposite ways: 1. Some speak about China from the point of view of China (their gaze coming from the inside), 2. Others deal with China from the point of view of the West. The philosopher suggests that "The right gaze is a sideways gaze" (2012: 177). One of the main problems of preparation is that we are forced to objectivise self and other, to label each other while 'humiliating' one of us (see microaggressions above, but from a broader perspective, e.g. in educational discourses). Metaphorically, gazing sideways represents an important effort to try to deal with interculturality from a new perspective that does not 'aggress' the Other with a direct gaze. By gazing sideways 'towards the Other' and attempting to leave aside some of the 'gazes' we have been imposed on by education, we might be able to meet the Other in novel ways. Looking at the Other is something we can't avoid, however. For the philosopher Emmanuel Lévinas (1906–1995):

> Firstly there is the straightness of the face, its directness, its defence-lessness. The skin of the face is at its most naked and defenceless. The most naked even though this nudity is decent. The most defenceless too: the face carries within it a certain poverty; the proof of that is that we try to mask this poverty by assuming poses, an attitude. The face is exposed, vulnerable, as if inviting an act of violence.
>
> (Lévinas, 1985: 112)

When I gaze sideways (metaphorically) during intercultural encounters, I need to look at the 'defenceless' face of the Other from a non-direct way, beyond the ideologies, the (hidden) dislike/hatred (often disguised under ethnocentrism) and the educational *prêt-à-penser* that are in me. I have always been inspired by the fact that the Finnish word for face is in fact plural: *Kasvot*. So, when I talk about my face in Finnish, I refer to it as 'my faces'. It is these *kasvot*, the plurality of the Other's face (as well as mine), that could guide my approach to interculturality. I must be unprepared to face these *kasvot* gazing sideways, in order to reconsider how we meet each other.

When we look into the eyes of the Other, we know that we don't know who they are, and that we will (maybe) never know. At the same time, we become aware of the fact that we cannot know who we are either – since we need that Other, whom we cannot know, to be someone. In the novel *The Idiot* (2001: 553), the character named Fyodorovitch exclaims: "To achieve perfection, one must first begin by not understanding many things! And if we understand too quickly, we may not understand well". Interculturality is 'a state of perfection' that we can never reach because it has to be renegotiated permanently with those we encounter. Education forces us, in a sense, to believe 1. in the idea that interculturality can be achieved through going up different levels of 'awareness', 'knowledge', 'transformation', etc. and 2. that we can 'force' a certain type of interaction and adaption onto the Other, the way we want it to be, the way the powers-that-be through education impose it to be in order to control the Other, to control interculturality. We (the Other and I) then have the illusion that we understand what is happening, often *quickly* because we are urged to do it 'quickly' and 'effectively'. However, in agreement with Dostoevsky's character, *we must not understand many things . . .* unpreparing to be prepared includes *non-understanding*, i.e. not knowing what is happening or why someone is behaving in certain ways. These mysteries go hand in hand with the plurality of the face that I encounter, which I will never be able to grasp fully – again: *I can't know what that face is gazing at in me and what hides behind these eyes that I look into.* Non-understanding should be integral to interculturality. I must accept that I can't know, and thus that I am not in control. Writer Xiaolu Guo (2020: 48) puts it nicely when she makes a character say: "(I feel) like a fish swimming in a new part of the ocean, unable to recognise the seaweed". I must accept that I cannot feed on something that I can't identify.

Yet, we can always try to be with the Other. Antoine de Saint-Exupéry's *The Little Prince* (1943/1971) will provide us with a first answer (a necessarily unsatisfactory answer). In the novella, the little boy meets a fox in Chapter 21. When he asks the fox to play with him, the fox says he cannot because he is not 'tamed' and suggests that the little boy 'tames him'. There is a slight difference of connotation between the English verb *to tame someone* (to bring under control) and its French equivalent *apprivoiser quelqu'un* (to domesticate) used in the original version. However, both mark unbalanced power relations, whereby one 'takes over' and reshapes the Other by taming them. As noted on several occasions in this book, a lot of intercultural encounters lead to these phenomena – ignoring the *inter-* of interculturality. Interestingly, when the fox explains what "tame me" means to the little boy, his explanation differs from the dictionary definition of the verb (Saint-Exupéry, 1943/1971: 65–66). He says:

> "It is an act too often neglected," said the fox. "It means to establish ties" . . . "To me, you are still nothing more than a little boy who is just

like a hundred thousand other little boys. And I have no need of you. And you, on your part, have no need of me. To you, I am nothing more than a fox like a hundred thousand other foxes. But if you tame me, then we shall need each other. To me, you will be unique in all the world. To you, I shall be unique in all the world".

For the fox, *to be tamed* means for both of those involved to start seeing the Other as 'unique in all the world'. When urged to explain how to do it concretely, the fox explains (Saint-Exupéry, 1943/1971: 67):

> "You must be very patient," replied the fox. "First you will sit down at a little distance from me – like that – in the grass. I shall look at you out of the corner of my eye, and you will say nothing. Words are the source of misunderstandings. But you will sit a little closer to me, everyday".

Patience, distance and trying to get a little closer to each other appear to be good advice to unprepare since these words are never used in education to describe the (imaginary) process of interculturality that students are meant to experience. These three words also question the illusion of closeness (the fox does not say *sit 'entirely' with each other at the end of the process*, but *a little closer everyday*) and urgency that educational discourses of interculturality systematically contain.

I have been reading a lot about composing and music playing recently. On many occasions, I have felt that what musicians say about their art is very relevant to unthink and rethink interculturality, and to try to be with the Other. Let me start with two composers of contemporary classical music: *Valentyn Silvestrov* (Ukraine) and *John Cage* (US). Both composers said similar things about the process of composing, which I am tempted to compare to interculturality here. Silvestrov (www.ecmrecords.com/art-ists/1435047071/valentin-silvestrov) explained: "I do not write new music. My music is a response to and an echo of what already exists". What Silvestrov means is that his music is influenced by the world around him, different sounds and voices and that it reflects these elements rather than create something that claims to be different. Like new music, interculturality, I believe, should be treated as both a response to and an echo of . . . sociality (be it intercultural or something else) – and not something else, something that we create artificially.[3] Earlier in this chapter, I maintained that, as social beings, we (are) prepare(d) to meet others from day one. Sociality is part of us. Meeting different others is a daily basic task for all of us. This means that processes of interculturality are also based on and reminiscent of these previous encounters that we have experienced ourselves or (actively/passively) witnessed (for example in a film). So, we do not need to rewrite interculturality every time we 'do' it, but we replay it based on past encounters – although they may sound/look different. I can see someone I have met before, who might be labelled (wrongly) as a 'non-intercultural' Other, in an 'intercultural' Other. The echo they create in us might trigger certain attitudes and behaviours in front of this new other. The face of the Other is a mystery; however, ways of meeting them are influenced by previous encounters (intercultural or not). Similar to Silverstrov, John Cage (in Cage & Goldberg, 1976: 104), who was a student of the Austrian composer Arnold Schoenberg (1874–1951), remembers that Schoenberg told him: "My purpose in teaching you is to make it impossible for you to write music". This meant: *writing music is something you have to learn by yourself. If I teach you, you will fail.* This contradictory and somewhat surprising statement also applies to interculturality and complements Silverstrov's assertion: If one is taught interculturality, one will not be able to 'do' interculturality, since the way it is taught will influence encounters and make interculturality 'ordered', 'programmed' and thus *un-intercultural*. Unpreparing would then mean leaving 'taught' interculturality behind and just letting it happen, as an echo of and response to students' (already) well-established (and often very complex) sociality.

My next inspiration comes from conducting music. We shall listen to what French conductor and composer Pierre Boulez (1925–2016) had to say about his profession. A conductor's task is to stress the musical pulse of e.g. an orchestra, a chorus, etc. so that the musicians can perform a musical piece together. This extremely complex task requires that the way the conductor has 'imagined' the musical piece to sound must be negotiated with every single musician to perform it. Boulez has taught conducting around the world and seems to agree with most people teaching conducting: there is not one model of a conductor because every single conductor has their own ways – as much as there is not one type of 'intercultural communicator'. About the use of hands and/or of a baton to conduct, he explains (1996: 64):

> The relationship between music and gesture has a physiological aspect that depends on each individual. Karajan [a famous Austrian conductor, 1908–1989] conducted with very rounded gestures, whereas Solti's are extremely angular. Both obtained the results they wanted . . . each technique has its merits – the resulting interpreting does not sound any better or worse because the conductors' gestures are angular or rounded.

Boulez (1996: 65) adds that, on several occasions, he has observed students trying to copy a certain style (e.g. Karajan's) but "It was utterly useless;

there was the outward form of his gestures, but not their essence". Meeting an Other, 'doing' interculturality also requires individual approaches to sociality to emerge. Often, in education, students are made to copy styles of communication, ways of meeting Others, which can make interculturality too programmed, artificial and ineffective. I remember listening to an English debate competition in China, where the students were merely 'parroting' the 'American' (a representation of it) accent, corporate nonverbality, the 'American' (a representation of it) way of presenting and humoring – which left me with an impression of drama, inauthenticity and frustration. This was interculturality without its *inter-* and *-ality* – a carbon copy of an imagined American style.

Boulez (1996: 89) also commented on the process of conducting an orchestra with 'famous' soloists:

In in the major orchestras, you deal with major soloists. You have to perform with them, not rap out orders as if they were babies. They're accomplished musicians and they have their own ideas. If they have achieved that stature, it's usually because they have great ability. So you must never try to dictate to them in any way at all. You simply listen to what they do and if you like it you don't need to say anything. If you find that a passage doesn't correspond at all to what you believe suits the ensemble, then you say, "I prefer this" and you work it out between you. There's a relationship of mutual consent, of give-and-take, between the person conducting and whoever is playing, especially a soloist.

Once again, I see this as a potential link to unpreparing for interculturality. I start from the assumption that everybody is a 'major' soloist in intercultural encounters, since, as social beings, we all have to deal with meeting Others all the time. No one can claim to be perfect or bad at it – this is counter-intuitive as, through education, we are made to believe that some are better than others, but I will stick to my guns and disagree. Sometimes we (believe that we) succeed, other times we (believe that we) fail. However, we (should) (are) all engage(d) in doing what Boulez describes between a conductor and a 'famous' soloist: "There's a relationship of mutual consent, of give-and-take". We try to "work it out between [us]". In order to achieve this, we need once again to be unprepared, to stop believing that we – or our interlocutors – are good and/or bad communicators because we are (randomly) *non-native speakers, young, old, female, queer, Japanese, Italian*, etc. (reasons that I have heard over the years). We need to put behind our beliefs about who the Other is based on hearsay, ethnocentrism, stereotypes or structurally racist ideologies and start trusting them to be as 'major' as we are in communicating. Finally, Boulez's words remind us that there is not one (perfect) way of playing a piece of music, as much as there is not just one way of doing interculturality. That is why I believe we need to move away from ready-made recipes offered by e.g. models of intercultural competence.

To conclude this section, let me share a final vision from the music world for unpreparing for interculturality. The American composer La Monte Young and visual artist Marian Zazeela set up a project called *The Dream House* in lower Manhattan, New York, US, in 1993. This sound and light environment combines purple and magenta lights, the aroma of incense, sustained pitches and music performed by live musicians at undetermined times. *The Dream House* is opened to the public and has functioned 24 hours a day since 1993. The musicians live in the house, perform whenever and for how long they wish in shifts, thus becoming natural components of the environment at their own will. For the composers, music does not have an end or a beginning and should thus be played continuously (with the help of technology). I see *The Dream House* as another potential metaphor for interculturality: as a phenomenon, interculturality has no beginning and no end, and like the musicians of the *Dream House*, we should feel comfortable enough to enter its realm, to contribute to it and to be part of it, whenever we want.

Figure 4.2 summarises the main points I made about *preparing to be unprepared* for interculturality:

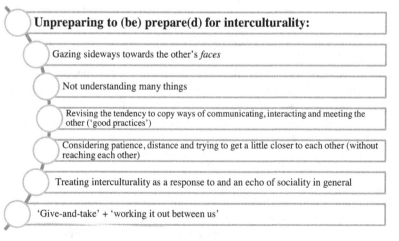

*Figure 4.2* Unpreparing to (be) prepare(d) for interculturality

**(A.S.)**

> Fear is a bad counsellor, but it makes us see many things we pretended not
> to see.
>
> (Agamben, 2020)

> My domestic worker, a very good-natured woman, is convinced that the
> epidemic was schemed by the "Arabs", by which I suppose she means the
> Muslims. Whether we're influenced by our small parish or by Carl Schmitt,
> whether ignorant or extremely learned, many of us need to make up our own
> plague-spreaders.
>
> (Benvenuto, 2020)

## Rejecting liberal conceptualisations of interculturality

As I have asserted in the previous chapters, encounters and experiences
about interculturality are simulations: we recreate and reimpose images,
icons and discourses from pervious experiences with, and through, others. Original images, icons and discourses become displaced by simulacra,
leaving superimposed copies whose images burn much brighter than the
original. I reject *the simulacrum of the liberal interculturalist* which has
dominated scholarship, research and teaching about intercultural communication education over the past few decades. The problematique that one
needs to directly address about *the liberal interculturalist* lies at the crux of
understanding how intercultural encounters and events are experienced and
understood. This is a primary problem at the heart of intercultural competencies (and the synonyms of other competencies such as global competence
and democratic competence). In previous publications, Fred and I (Simpson
and Dervin, 2019a; 2019b; 2019c) have warned against Anglo-centric and
Euro-centric supranational models of interculturality due to the fact that
the universalism (the idea that that some ideas have universal application
or applicability) these models argue for is conceptually impotent: exclusion cannot be eradicated as universalism in itself engenders an 'us' versus
'them' praxis.

In this sense, the quote from Agamben at the start of this section is poignant as it seemingly runs contra to the ideological impositions of liberal
interculturalism. The point here is that fear(s) are inescapable and are an
operative function in how one understands one's self and that of the other.
Often, our gravest fears are seen exclusively in the other. Thus, simply the
self 'becoming other' through discourses and representations of being 'more
respectful', 'more tolerant' or 'more open' (being the liberal interculturalist par excellence) are rendered obsolete by the (self's perceived) fears
which suffocate the other. There is another point to be made here, regarding

the quantitative assessment of intercultural competence. One might score very highly in a degree module/training programme/specialised course on intercultural competence, one even may get a certificate or qualification from such courses or programmes.[4] But what does this really mean? One cannot master interculturality because interculturality is always in the making. *The liberal interculturalist simulacrum* here gives the false impression that interculturality can be 'obtained' or 'acquired' as a goal or achievement. Thus, it becomes a fixed state attributed to one's being (i.e. that one is supposed or *ought* to *be*, speak, act or think in a particular way which is supposed to be 'intercultural' or that one is in some capacity an 'expert' at interculturality). But what if the scenarios, tasks or examinations contained in the assessment of interculturality were simulated? There are two points to be made here: Firstly, answers and responses can be simulated to relate to dominant ideological positions. How does one, for example, assess 'tolerance' or 'respect' as they are inherently subjective notions? Any attempt to impose these notions as fixed universalist entities strips the notions bare of the possibility of the plurality of meaning (in many contexts around the world, there are often multiple meanings, and certain words do not correspond to a particular English word whereby equivalence can never be realised). Secondly, the self can simulate particular forms of discourses and images that function as a masquerade: the person becomes an expert by getting an A grade in intercultural competence yet their self contains racist sentiments and xenophobia towards the other. The point is one cannot know whether someone is telling the 'truth' or not. For example, perhaps some students will say or do what the teacher/lecturer wants to hear to get 'good grades' in programmes/courses/modules on interculturality.

I would argue the current coronavirus pandemic is an example *par excellence* of the fallacy of the liberal interculturalist: that interculturality cannot be obtained or acquired by the self. At a time when humanity is supposedly 'the most global' and 'the most open' it has ever been, this convergence lies with neoliberal economic-political dominance over life, with its ideologies of individual freedom, respect and tolerance. Yet, as Fred succinctly notes in his earlier sections, the racism, xenophobia and Sinophobia which have become evident throughout the pandemic reflect something somewhat different in reality. The second quotation from Sergio Benvenuto is especially relevant here. One needs to urgently think and rethink: How are our own 'plague-spreaders' produced and reproduced? And, why are our own 'plague-spreaders' produced and reproduced? I will elaborate on these musings later in this section in relation to the coronavirus pandemic of 2020.

A simple answer to whether can we (get) prepared for interculturality would be no. As I have stated in previous sections, the self can never actualise a stable relationship with the other because we have no way of knowing what the other demands from us, and we have no way of knowing what the other can see, think and so forth. Yet, this has not stopped the field of intercultural communication education from proposing ways to get prepared for interculturality, in different and similar guises, for the best part of 70 years. I am not limiting a specific temporal historicity upon interculturality as the other has had different historical names, e.g. 'the Barbarian' in Ancient Greece', 'the savage' in the 17th century, and differing sociohistorical conceptualisations from context to context (see Dervin, 2016). If I am asserting that it is not possible to be prepared for interculturality, then the questions one needs to ask are: *How has the field constructed an assumption that one can be prepared for interculturality?*, and, *Why has the field been constructed upon the assumption that interculturality can be prepared for?* With the specific focus on intercultural communication education scholarship, from Edward T Hall's *The Silent Language* (1959), Geert Hofstede's work on culture's consequences (1983), to Michael Byram's Intercultural Communicative Competence (1997), amongst others, the red thread that links these scholars is a preoccupation in how to engage with the other. In how the self can prepare to meet, greet, observe and speak to the other. There is a fatal distance here, between the self and the other, whose territory has been marked and remarked by different theoretical approaches to the study of intercultural communication education. The aspect that unites all of these approaches are founded upon and reproduce a separation between the human and the animal, which I call *the biopolitics of interculturality*.

## The biopolitics of everyday life

Biopolitical power refers to a power that is articulated in the production, management and administration of 'life'. An affirmative biopolitics is one that is "not defined negatively with respect to the *dispositifs* of modern power/knowledge but is rather situated along the line of tension that traverses and displaces them" (Esposito, 2012: 18). Biopolitics is a politics in the name for life whereas biopower refers to a life subjected to the command of politics (Esposito, 2008). For Roberto Esposito (2012: 12):

> Whether you choose to view the philosophy of the person as an unconscious (or even denied) form of biopolitics, or anti-personalist biopolitics as an inner fold of the *dispositif* of the person, either way we are defined by our relationship with the animal that both dwells inside us and alters us.

The root of the convergence is based on how the human is defined. For instance, in the Aristotelian sense, the human being as a rational animal. Esposito argues that because of the assumption that human beings are (assumed as being) rational the "biopolitical corporealization of the person and spiritualistic personalization of the body are inscribed inside the same theoretical circle" (Ibid.). Esposito shows how biological knowledge became mixed with philosophical and political thought from the 18th century onwards. The theory of a double biological layer within every living being – one vegetative and unconscious, and the other cerebral and relational – was first put forward by the French anatomist and pathologist Xavier Bichat (1771–1802) in the form of medical knowledge, then 'translated' by the German philosopher Arthur Schopenhauer (1788–1860) into philosophical knowledge and subsequently, by the French philosopher Auguste Comte (1798–1857) into sociological knowledge. For Esposito, the 1800s to the "emphatically racist anthropology of the 1900s" (Esposito, 2012: 7) resulted in anthroposociology: the anthropological and sociological study of race as a means of establishing the superiority of certain peoples and/or groups. Articulated in its turn in terms of comparative zoology, the animal thus became a point of division within humanity, between species of people who were separated by their relation to life (e.g. Social Darwinism: "the survival of the fittest" between difference races as a means to justify imperialism, racism, eugenics and social inequality).

In these logics, life and the person cannot *be* in co-existence as the person becomes defined by the distance that separates it from the body. To articulate this, Esposito (2012: 13) gives an example from Ancient Rome in terms of the separation between *persona* and *homo*: not all human beings are persons, neither are all persons human beings. The result is a hierarchy gradation of *full person, semi-person, non-person* and *anti-person* (represented by the adult, the infant or disabled adult, the incurably ill and the insane). Here, the state functions paternally through a personhood mechanism marking "the final difference between what must live and what can be legitimately cast to death" (Esposito, 2012: 13).

In his (2017) book *The Origin of the Political: Hannah Arendt Or Simone Weil?* Esposito, through the work of Simone Weil (1909–1943) exclaims, what is sacred in humans is not their *persona*, it is that which is not covered by their mask. Thus, "the neuter [neither masculine nor feminine grammatical forms] is not another person added to the first two, rather it is neither one nor the other and what defies all dichotomies founded on, or presupposed by, the language of the person" (Esposito, 2012: 16). In some fields of anthropology during the late 19th and early 20th century, the language of the person was exclusively determined by the biological conceptualisation of race. The person who ties the structure of a language to the biological substance of the race in an even tighter knot is the Belgian linguist Joseph Honoré Chavée (1815–1877), author of a text entitled

"Languages and Races". Esposito shows, through quoting Chavée, "'Every language", his opening statement declares, "is a natural complement to human organization that is anatomically, physiologically, and psychologically specialized to each race" (Esposito, 2012: 43) (e.g. Chavée gives the examples of the Chinese race to the Chinese language and the 'Indo-European'[5] race to the 'Indo-European' language). In this sense, in Bichat's canonical dual division (the vegetative and the unconscious), although language is meant for interhuman communication, its material structure makes it closer to 'organic life' than to 'animal life' (Esposito, 2012). Esposito argues that a third layer is constituted – a semantic side, divided into two, which preserves the soul of the word; and one of a syllabic body, which is destined to weaken and fall ill. Esposito argues the separation of the person from the animal

> also allowed him [Chavée] to rivet the relationship between languages – and therefore between races – to a comparative framework that did not move it upwards or downwards. Each language remains fixed in a hierarchical position which is determined by its inevitable racial association.
>
> (Esposito, 2012: 44)

To illuminate this example further, there is a poignant example from China in the early 20th century. The third edition (1910) of *A Great English-Chinese Dictionary* (whose first edition had been published in 1908), compiled by Yan Huiqing, notes, "But notably, the sample sentences in Yan's dictionary were already starting to use the most important antonyms of 'civilisation' and 'culture': 'barbarism' and 'savage(-ry),' as I 'from barbarism to civility' and 'the cultivation of savages'" (Fang, 2019: 80–81). Here, the language of culture becomes inscribed as a form of biopolitics. Culture becomes a dualist antonym of barbarism and savagery (e.g. China and her people are barbaric and need to become more civil like the 'West'), whereby modernist biopolitical power becomes a way to administer life over another population (in this example, China).

## The biopolitics of interculturality

Edward T Hall (1914–2009) worked at the US State Department Foreign Service Institute teaching communication skills to foreign service personnel and diplomats who were to be stationed in different contexts around the world. Hall is regarded as one of the founders of what today is known as the field of intercultural communication, and his work still remains popular amongst researchers and teachers of interculturality. Hall argues in

*The Silent Language* (1959) that two of the ultimate steps in analysing culture involve (1959: 50):

1     To identify the building blocks of culture – what we later came to call the isolates of culture, akin to the notes of a musical score
2     To tie these isolates into a biological base so that they could be compared among cultures. We also stipulated that this comparison be done in such a way that the conditions be repeatable at will. Without this, anthropology can lay no claim to being a science.

Hall goes on to argue that "culture is bio-basic – [it is] rooted in biological activities" (Hall, 1959: 60). For Hall there is no break between the past and the present, "the present, in which man acts as a culture producing animal, and the past, when there were no men and no cultures". (Ibid.)

Here, there is a chilling similarity in Esposito's critique of the biopolitics used by Nazi Germany:

> What kept the two types of human beings – superior and inferior – at an infinite distance was not only their difference in the present, but also their past and future differences. Just as the superior have no past, the inferior have no future. The superior have always come after the human, while the inferior have always come before the human and continue to do so.
>
> (Esposito, 2012: 45)

What is important to think about here is when Esposito argues the superior have no past, and Hall argues culture is rooted in the biological past, the lineage of both arguments converge upon the fact that this biological past is one of race as a biological construct. The superior has no past because they create and recreate myths about the contents and attributes of their dominance in the present. This body politic of dominance is vested in the present. Whereas the inferior remain the 'savagery' and 'barbarism' of the past, and it's their annihilation in the future the superior body politic is founded upon.

The convergence lies in how Hall continues the biopolitical separation between the life of the person and the life of the animal through the language of culture. The example here is what Esposito calls 'linguistic race', the notion that all languages degenerate whereby some degenerate quicker than others. In Hall's work (which contains very little use of the word 'race'), 'linguistic race' is substituted for 'linguistic culture' yet the remnants of this separation between the life of the person and the animal life remain. In quoting Benjamin Lee Whorf (1897–1941), readers might be aware of the Sapir-Whorf hypothesis and its historical influences on interculturality (e.g. Holliday et al., 2010). Hall and Trager (1953) presented a matrix for mapping culture along certain dimensions the most important of which was communication, both verbal and nonverbal. A concept that guided their work was the Sapir-Whorf hypothesis. The Sapir-Whorf hypothesis is a heavily criticised instrument for its emphasis on homogenous languages and 'cultures'. These same references are made in Hall's (1959) seminal work *The Silent Language* and in Hall and Trager's (1953) *Analysis of Culture*. Hall and Trager (1953) assert "the activities of living matter are functions neither of chance nor design, but of direct and dynamic interaction of the organism with its environment" (Hall and Trager, 1953: 7). In part, this quote is cited by Hall and Trager from the Russian-American Evolutionary Biologist Theodosius Dobzhansky (1900–1975) in his (1950) publication *The Genetic Basis of Evolution* and is based upon the genetic differences between different populations of peoples. Although Dobzhansky (1950) rejected the idea of a pure race as all races are constituted through what Dobzhansky calls mixing (Dobzhansky, 1950), there are a number of controversies about Dobzhansky's notion of race. From the time of Hall's (1959) work, a publication which is seen today as one of the foundations of intercultural communication, and is still widely used and venerated, *race functions as a proxy for population structure and control.* The fact is that Dobzhansky insisted throughout his career that there is such a thing as a legitimate biological concept of race (Gannett, 2013). Faber (2016: 627) argues, "Dobzhansky, relied heavily on the concept of 'subspecies' in his major works . . . and defended the use of 'race' in human classification". Dobzhansky, who is cited in Hall's work on culture, argues that racially distinct populations do exist due to evolutionary forces and genetic differences. There are a plethora of examples I could choose from to illustrate this. One can be found in Hall (1959: 146): "Americans and Spaniards at a bullfight provide a familiar example of how the same set of circumstances can be experienced differently". Here, nationality (even though Hall is referring to what he calls 'culture') incorporates the political-ideological body of the nation-state and becomes the sole factor and key determinant in ordering how experiences can be understood.

The modern-day apparatus of research and teaching on interculturality is built upon a *biopolitical apparatus of (biological) racial differences as cultural differences.* Race is often substituted today by 'culture'. This lineage continues the separation of the person and the animal. Instead of races being 'barbaric' or 'savage', now it is cultures who needed to become 'more civilised'. The difference in how the biopolitics of liberal approaches to interculturality have functioned over the past few decades lies in the shifting rhetorical devices whereby the other (on the surface) has gone from a 'savage' to the other who has 'cultural differences' which need to be 'understood', 'recognised and 'acknowledged', yet the biopolitical mechanism that underpins these forces remains the same: the separation of the personal from the animal. In *Postmodernity and Its Discontents* (1997), the Polish sociologist Zygmunt Bauman (1925–2017) argues "the typical modern strangers were the waste of the State's ordering zeal. What the modern strangers did not fit was the vision of order" (Bauman, 1997: 18). These functions resulted in differing strategies which were deployed to the stranger: *assimilation: making the different similar*; *devouring the other: annihilating the strangers by devouring them and then metabolically transforming into a tissue indistinguishable from one's own* (Ibid.). Other ordering structures included banishing and barring the other through exclusion and 'cleansing' the other – "expelling the strangers beyond the frontiers of the managed and manageable territory; or, when neither of the two measures was feasible – destroying the strangers physically" (Bauman, 1997: 18). These strategies have been employed over populations for centuries to counter the so-called 'barbaric', 'strangers', 'outliers' and so forth.

The biopolitics of interculturality is not a phantasm of the right/centre/left of the so-called 'political spectrum' – biopolitics permeates all aspects of life and death. As Esposito succinctly puts in *Bios: Biopolitics and Philosophy* (2008), "politics penetrates directly in life and life becomes other from itself" (Esposito, 2008: 15). It is at this juncture where Esposito argues that there is a biopolitical convergence and similarity in how both the biopolitics of Nazi Germany on one hand, and liberalism on the other, function similarly. Esposito argues,

> actually it becomes even more evident – that the reasoning behind the relationship thus established between body and thing is in any case analogous: if you start from an instrumental conception of life – whether enlisted in the service of the sovereign state or of the individual – the condition of one tends to slide into that of the other.
>
> (Esposito, 2012: 91)

For liberalism, the person owns their body themselves. Ownership is inscribed to the person inside the body (e.g. as opposed to Nazism where the body is owned by the body of state sovereignty). However, Esposito shows the semblance of Nazi biopolitics and liberal biopolitics insofar,

> what makes these perspectives overlap or intersect through a somewhat similar conceptual vocabulary is the animalization or reification of one area of the human over another, which is simultaneously opposed to it and superimposed on it.
>
> (Esposito, 2012: 91)

The problem is liberalism's basis on rationalism: the individual's mind is placed as being sovereign over the whole of the person. The sovereignty of the mind is placed over the body – the body becomes a dominion to the mind. Thus, the *dispositif* of the person functions as personalisation (in the rational part) and toward depersonalisation (in the animal or bodily part). Thus, "conversely, a person is a person if it reduces to thingness that out of which it arises on the basis of its own rational-spiritual status" (Esposito, 2012: 92). It is these never-ending, continual and uninterrupted processes which engender the other.

There is an important point to be made here: the *liberal interculturalist simulacrum* must be rejected in its entirety. My argument here is, *the liberal interculturalist* conception of life, based upon individual rationality and universalism. The vocabulary that one needs to be 'respectful', 'tolerant', 'open' to the other reproduces the other through this particular categorical language of the person. To put this another way, 'respect', 'tolerance', 'openness' become normative objects in which the person recreates their own myths, phantasms and ideologies about these notions, which in turn are oriented towards what they are not, *an other*. At the same time, the person becomes the likeness of the thing (respect, tolerance), because the mind (rationalism) dominates the body, thus the person attributes the thing to their own personal sovereignty (e.g. the self may say things such as, "I am the most tolerant of people from other contexts", "I hold no racist views", "I hold no stereotypes towards people from context x"). The fundamental problem with liberal approaches to interculturality is that because the conceptual basis is founded upon rationalism, the self assumes that it can prepare for interculturality, because the self thinks it has 'mastered' or has full knowledge about its own sense of being, which is always contra to the other, contra to what the self thinks it is not. This assumption reproduces the duality that the self is dominant over (or even better than) the other. Thus, the *liberal interculturalist* becomes seduced by their own rational-spiritual status, by their own ego.

## Biopolitics, interculturality and coronavirus

This chapter started with the question: Can we (get) prepared for interculturality? The example *par excellence* that one cannot get prepared for interculturality is the current coronavirus pandemic. The final section of this chapter will offer a short commentary on some of the notions discussed in this chapter in relation to the coronavirus pandemic.

As the media reporting commenced about the initial stages of the virus (I am writing this chapter in the late summer of 2020), my initial musings were drawn to *The European Journal of Psychoanalysis*, which was running an on-going edition *Coronavirus and Philosophers* from February 2020 to April 2020, inviting philosophers to post their early reflections on COVID-19, response to criticisms of their arguments or to post amendments/clarifications of their arguments. The philosophers included G. Agamben, J.L. Nancy, R. Esposito, S. Benvenuto, D. Dwivedi, S. Mohan, R. Ronchi, & M. de Carolis (see www.journal-psychoanalysis.eu/coronavirus-and-philosophers/). I am particularly interested in the first edition, since there have been two further editions on *Psychoanalysis Facing Coronavirus* and *Enduring Pandemic: Further Transmissions from Psychoanalysts and Philosophers.*

In a short article titled *Vitam Instituere*, Roberto Esposito (2020) argues "at a time when human life appears to be threatened and overpowered by death, our common effort can only be that of 'establishing' it again and again". *Vitam Instituere* of the Roman period delineates the unchanging horizon of institutional montages (Goodrich, 1997). Perhaps one example of the current pandemic can be found in how early in 2020 (especially in the European context) initial responses included "oh it's just like influenza", "it's not so serious" and so forth. The subsequent institutional montages that re-established life again and again (when the pandemic turned out to be more and more serious, when it got out of control), became that the other is a problem, it is the other that has caused the coronavirus. Often, these representations included xenophobic, racist and Sinophobic representations about China and her people. Here, the biopolitical montage of life establishing itself again and again – was, and is, engendered through the same biopolitical apparatus deployed under (liberal) modernity – the other is savage, the other is barbaric (e.g. "the Chinese people who ate at the 'supposed' outbreak starting point in the Wuhan market are 'barbaric', 'savage', etc.).

In the current time of coronavirus, Esposito makes the argument that,

> at a time when we are doing all that is in our power to stay alive, as is understandable, we cannot renounce the second life – life with others, for others, through others. This is not, however, allowed, in fact it is, rightly and logically, forbidden.
>
> (Esposito, 2020)

To put this another way, especially in light of the situation at the end of summer 2020, in an ontological and practical sense, the other, and the others we interact with, cannot be negated and forbidden. If the other is negated or forbidden, it would place me outside of myself: the death of the other is what cannot be experienced (i.e. death itself) (Esposito, 2010). At a time when everyone everywhere is being submitted to differing and similar forms of death, the (perceived) death of certain imaginaries (of globalisation, of neo-liberalism, of hypermobility, free movement), fears about death itself (the loss of loved ones, family members, friends, colleagues) and even the (perceived) death of certain identities (local, national, global) "because of the other", institutional montages (*Vitam Instituere*) constitute our conceptualisation of life and death. Yet, as I have shown, the biopolitics which runs through these apparatuses are based upon culturalist and anthropocentric prejudice. The other will always be other.

On the current coronavirus pandemic, the philosopher Rocco Ronchi makes the provocative and important argument that,

> Our culturalist and anthropocentric prejudice was not overcome by the slow and almost always ineffective action of education: a cough was enough to make it suddenly impossible to evade the responsibility that each individual has towards all living beings for the simple fact of (still) being part of this world, and of wanting to be part of it.
>
> (Ronchi, 2020)

The implication, in light of the current pandemic, is with regard to the ethical reciprocity of the self and the other. As I have argued in previous chapters of this book, which is also relevant to interculturality in the time of coronavirus, is that there is an urgent need to (re)connect the self in dialogue with the other through an ontological approach based upon non-normative dialogical ethics. The ground of *svoboda* (freedom) is a site to do this whereby the self and others, through co-being and co-existence, interact in a state of reciprocity. It is on that structure that the free (ethical) act (*postupok*) [поступок] is ultimately based. There is thus no alibi about coronavirus or interculturality because there is no alibi in Being. To paraphrase Vasylchenko (2014: 1106), one must choose between the caritas of total responsibility for oneself and the universe, on the one hand, and the total diabolical destruction of "everything is permitted" on the other. The important point here, is that currently, towards the end of the summer of 2020, with regard to the coronavirus pandemic and with regard to interculturality, *currently everything is not permitted*. We are required to act immediately and decisively (even though not all actors have done so). The Indian philosophers Divya Dwivedi and Shaj Mohan (2020) make an important argument about coronavirus insofar that one is seized by responsibility when one is confronted with an individual life which is in the seizure of death. In the sense that death and responsibility go together.

The institutional montages that re-establish life again and again (through the biopolitics of modernity) need to be decentred and destabilised. The biopolitics of liberal modernity, which, as I have shown, is also found at the heart of theoretical and practical approaches about interculturality, must be abandoned due to their inherently racist mechanisms. These montages will continue to replicate the other as the savage and barbarian, today and tomorrow, just like they were yesterday. The rhetorical devices used may shift, but the underlying biopolitical apparatus will remain the same: the separation of the person from the animal. At the heart of interculturality, the *biopolitical apparatus of (biological) racial differences as cultural differences* is shown today through the racism and discrimination attributed to 'cultural difference' discourses. The current coronavirus pandemic has merely removed the veiled cloak from these issues which have been masquerading as 'respect' and 'tolerance' for decades. For both research and teaching, the ethical act must commence now. This movement lies in going beyond liberal interculturalist approaches as a matter of urgency.

## [Synopsis]

In this chapter, we both agree that preparing and/or being prepared for interculturality is impossible and attempts to do so must be rejected.

Meeting the Other is always enigmatic since we cannot know who this Other *really* is, what they *really* want from and demand from us and vice versa. Even those we think we know, maybe we don't know. Since interculturality is always in the making, we cannot 'control' it, even if we are 'ordered' to do so (*"tolerate!"*, *"respect!"*). We are already all used to meeting strangers on a daily basis, in our own surroundings, with whom we must live, work or study. The strategies we develop, test and re-use might also be useful to meet interculturally. We also both insist on one central aspect of human interaction, which is performance and play. Since these are so important in sociality, they make us question certain claims that are often expected of 'interculturally competent' individuals such as "I have a lot of respect for their culture", "I have no stereotypes about the Chinese", "I am not a racist", etc.

Liberal conceptualisations of interculturality, however, force us to believe that we can prepare for meeting interculturally. Models of intercultural competence from the West, *biopolitical apparatuses of (biological) racial differences as cultural/linguistic differences*, create this simulacrum and fool us into believing that we can reach better levels of interculturality with the Other. What is then interesting is to examine how and why interculturalists have constructed the idea that we can be prepared for interculturality. Whose voice(s) dominate in this doxa? And whose voice(s) are marginalised?

While Fred suggests ways of unpreparing to (be) prepare(d) for interculturality by accepting that we cannot understand everything and gazing sideways towards the Other's faces, Ashley proposes (re)connecting through an ontological approach based upon non-normative dialogical ethics.

## [Going further]

The question of preparation for interculturality is one of the most central topics in education for diversity. After reading this chapter, reflect on these questions:

- What is the etymology and archeology of the verb *to meet* in English and the other languages that you know? What do they reveal about the idea of encounters?
- Have you ever taken part in some form of preparation for interculturality? What was it like? What did you learn?
- Which models of intercultural competence are you aware of? What do you know about the way they were created? What do you know about the authors? What ideologies do they represent? How do you feel about these ideologies?
- Why is it that supranational institutions like the European Union or the UNESCO support research on intercultural competence and produce models? Do you think that they have hidden agendas?
- How could you unprepare to (get) prepare(d)? What from your own knowledge of intercultural encounters should you revise to unprepare?
- What do you think of the argument that meeting interculturally is the same as meeting people 'intraculturally'?

## Notes

1 I put *polite* between inverted commas since the term refers to different realities in different contexts, with different people. For instance, not asking "How are you?" in English is not a sign of impoliteness or bad manners interculturally speaking.
2 Chinese people are often classified as collectivistic amongst interculturalists. In their book entitled *iChina: The Rise of the Individual in Modern Chinese Society*, Hansen & Svarverud (2010) (eds.) show otherwise.
3 I have been struggling to understand for example the difference between so-called 'intracultural' and 'intercultural' communication, which I think is an artificial dichotomy.
4 See for example The Certificate for Intercultural Competence (ZERTIKO) at Humbolt University in Berlin (Germany).
5 About the myth of the 'Indo-European' race/language, see Demoule (2017).

# 5 What is the state of research on interculturality today?

## (F.D.)

In this chapter, we discuss the situation of research on interculturality. Adopted in the 1950s in communication studies, then in education in the 1970s and in other fields of research since the 1990s, the field of all things related to interculturality is a complex one. It is hard to say what it includes and excludes since some fields might focus on the notion but under other labels (e.g. global, cross-cultural). Looking at my own publications, they have been mostly included in the broad fields of communication, applied linguistics and education, in some parts of the world, while excluded in others. Some have also found their way in other fields (e.g. migration studies, anthropology). So, when I talk about intercultural research here, I am not too sure what it is that I refer to. The comments I will make below about the state of research on interculturality are necessarily limited and might refer to branches of interculturality that have to do with 1. preparing people for interculturality (e.g. language education, health care studies) and 2. analysing the intercultural experiences of mobile and migrant individuals (e.g. higher education, business studies). Regardless of the field, those involved in researching interculturality might face the problems that I highlight below. I remind the reader that my contexts of practice and research are today essentially Finland and Mainland China. In the past, I have been involved with scholars and educators in Australia, France, Iceland, Malaysia, Sweden, Switzerland, the UK, the US and marginally Israel and Luxembourg.

The first element that we need to bear in mind when we think about research on interculturality is that it seems to have now reached *global audiences* of teachers, researchers and students. By saying that, I am not claiming that *it is global* in the sense that it would include multiple ways of thinking about it. It is only global by the amount of research, publications and courses that are shared by scholars from around the world. The second remark that I wish to make is that the field of interculturality (or the fields that relate to interculturality), like all other fields, is clearly embedded in the global corporate identity of today's academia. It means that the knowledge that is produced about it, the training that is 'sold' about it in higher education and 'outsourced' for the general public (e.g. through open universities, courses sold to companies), the publications produced about it and the funding scholars apply for are all part of the global money-making world of academia. An idea (ideology), a concept, a model of intercultural competence, an 'order' about how to do interculturality or a research paper are all potential contributors to increasing financial capitals for institutions and for some, for the 'fame' of individual scholars and/or teachers themselves. This important aspect, which is rarely discussed, not only has an influence on the output (again: research papers, models of training), on the ideologies that are preferred and promoted in relation to interculturality in a given context, but also on the education and training of individuals and on the broader society.

In what follows, I propose a list of concrete problems that I have noticed through my engagement with hundreds of different kinds of scholars, through reading the literature, reviewing hundreds of research papers and books and attending conferences around the world.

There are artificial boundaries between the different fields of research that work on intercultural issues. Scholars get labelled (or label themselves with a sense of pride sometimes) as educationalists, communication specialists or 'language people' and rarely get to enter into meaningful dialogues with each other. That said, some 'big gurus' get quoted and used in different fields of research related to interculturality when their models have reached a certain fame (Bennett, Byram, Deardorff, etc.). Unfortunately, their models become a-contextualised and generally applied to any context of interculturality. For example, I attended a PhD defense once during which the candidate discussed their use of M. Bennett's Developmental *Model* of Intercultural Sensitivity (DMIS) (Bennett, 1986) for examining school children according to their faiths. I was not too convinced by the use of this model, especially as the candidate seemed to take it for granted that it was adapted to their specific context of study and research problem – although it was developed in the US and contains clear neoliberal ideologies.

The use of concepts in the field of interculturality is also a problem. Concepts are sometimes borrowed from other fields, but with a somewhat delay in the way they are problematised, understood and used – interculturalists not always being aware of their archaeologies. There are clear trends. Overnight, promoted by a 'famous' scholar or a supranational institution, a concept or a notion shoots to fame. This has been the case of concepts such as (randomly) 'citizenship', 'contact zones', 'cosmopolitanism', 'decolonising', 'third space', 'social justice' and 'translanguaging'. Concepts are obviously essential to research. However, when they are used without any awareness of the ideologies that hide behind them, their histories or their meanings in different fields and languages, this cannot really lead to advancing the field of interculturality.

A major problem with research on interculturality – and I have discussed this extensively in previous chapters – rests on the omnipresence and control exercised by Western English-speaking scholars. In a forthcoming paper, R'boul shows how the majority of editors and editorial board members of the three most important international journals of intercultural communication are based mostly in the US, Europe, Australia and New Zealand. Representation from Africa for example is only 0.86% (R'boul, forth.).

Their voices are to be found globally, hardly ever questioned and 'recycled' without meaningful discussions – as if their 'truth' was the only 'truth'. Since they publish in top journals, with top international publishers and are invited as keynote speakers for top international conferences, their voices are omnipresent and deemed to be powerful. The fact that supranational institutions pay them to produce models of intercultural competence, in which they embed certain economic-political ideologies, is also noteworthy. For instance, I find using the idea of 'intercultural citizenship', which was 'invented' in a specific European context, in Mainland China problematic. Potentially, the concept could be given a different meaning in this context (revised and enriched?), but when it is taken for granted as it stands in its Eurocentric package, it does not seem to make much sense. I have also noticed that in 'voiceless' contexts – meaning contexts to which the powerful never really give the floor to enrich and/or question their ideologies – there are gatekeepers who were educated in the US and the UK. What I mean is, some scholars in the 'periphery' flood their market with these Western ideologies, present them as the one and only 'truth' about interculturality and close the door to potential meaningful (not just decorative) enrichment and questioning – looking down upon local scholars and educators who are dissatisfied with these ideologies.[1] Yet, they might allow, for example, the combination of 'ancient' local philosophical knowledge treated a-historically (e.g. a clichéd Confucian concept, whose essence has been purged) and Byram's ideas. For example from a Chinese perspective, although they are the basis of today's Chinese society, there hasn't been – to my knowledge – any attempt at combining Marxist-Leninist ideologies with Western gurus' ideas – or substituting them. When Mei Yuan and I suggested using the phrase Minzu education in English to refer to 'Chinese ethnic minority education', and to offer an alternative to European intercultural education, a UK-educated Chinese gatekeeper told us: "you can't use this phrase in research in English; we all call it *ethnic minority education*". I tried to explain that the phrase *ethnic minority* in English does not connote the same as Minzu in Chinese, and that it gives a wrong economic-political impression of China to those who don't know the context – but to no good, they would not listen. *Americans call it ethnic minority education so it should be so!* This gatekeeper's problem, I realised, was their lack of knowledge about what Minzu education is about and their own fantasy about fearing political repression.

We could rejoice that, at times, a name from outside the 'West' appears in research of interculturality. However, I feel that these names are often used as tokens to show '(false) generosity' and perform interculturality within interculturality. But I am not always convinced that their voices are taken seriously and that the floor is given to them genuinely. What is more, many of these voices tend to speak with and for the powerful voices, not always attempting to try to add to or question them. Finally, many of them were trained in the 'West' and might be tempted to mimic Western 'prêt-à-penser' about interculturality to get published in top Western journals.

In the previous chapter, I discussed the problem of education giving us 'invisible' orders as to how we should do interculturality and thus meet other people. Obviously, the influence of research on this is immense. By listing the *knowledge, attitudes, skills of interpreting and relating*, and even anything that contains the word *critical* as in *critical awareness*, researchers involved in education for interculturality do give orders to those who (have to) listen to them. Their dreams, their fantasies, their political beliefs (and belongings in many cases) and their own imaginaries lead the world to 'do' interculturality. When researchers are given so much power, with neither critique (or very little) nor resistance from other scholars and educators, it becomes a problem for interculturality. As I said earlier, we work on a notion that requires us to look for diversity, real opportunities for deep (and not necessarily easy) dialogues and to fight against inequality, but we deal with it theoretically, conceptually and methodologically without the *inter-* of interculturality. One geographical location (Europe or the US, marginally Australia and Canada) decides.

In recent years, there has been a lot of discussions around the concept of *microaggressions*. Sue (2010: 5) defines the concept as follows: "the brief and commonplace daily verbal, behavioral, and environmental indignities, whether intentional or unintentional, that communicate hostile, deroga-tory, or negative racial, gender, sexual-orientation, and religious slights and insults to the target person or group". Behind the ideologies that 'gov-ern' research on intercultural communication education hide what I would call 'legitimised microaggressions': (disguised) stereotyping (heard from a Finnish teacher: "how do your people celebrate New Year?"), imposi-tion of cultural difference (heard from another Finnish teacher in front of a class with one migrant child: "we Finns are hardworking and brave"), essentialist pedagogical differentialism (heard repeatedly about Chinese students in the 'West': "they have no sense of critical thinking, so they don't need to do this exercise"), (hidden) politicisation of interculturality (heard at a Finnish university: "we will support students from countries like China that do not have democracy and human rights"), etc. Often, the recipients of such fantasised discourses do experience 'fatigue' of these legalised microaggressions. Research on interculturality also often creates such microaggressions. In an article in 2012, I showed that many papers written by White English-speaking scholars had used incomplete and stereotypical knowledge about Confucianism to describe the experience of Chinese students in Australia, New Zealand and the UK (Dervin, 2012). This is obviously problematic as it gave very negative pictures of the 'Chinese student', who, by means of faulty interpretations of Confucianism, was said to be a-critical, 'stuffed ducks' in the classroom, and overly respectful of authority. A Chinese student reading the papers might experience them as microaggressions.

These are the main problems I see with research on interculturality today. Obviously, many more issues have been discussed in length in previous sections.

I would now like to share some reflections on how we could try to limit the problems highlighted above:

Let me start with this quote from the French poet, writer and philosopher Paul Valéry (1871–1945): "What has always been accepted by everyone, everywhere, is almost certain to be wrong" (our translation, 1943: 452). *Question! Question! Question! Never be satisfied with one ideology. Scholarship on interculturality should never stop un-re-thinking.*

Reading interdisciplinarily should help us avoid anachronic (and thus acritical) ideologies of interculturality. *We must dig into the archeology of things.*

As noted on several occasions in this book, what I have learnt through the years is that research on interculturality is partly some form of *theatocracy*: only 'powerful' voices arrange and organise power within the field (white English-speakers) while often pretending to be generous with others. I suspect that, by engaging with powerful decision makers, big publishing companies, who determine their research discourses, ideologies and agendas, we become limited in the way they modify the way they construct and present interculturality. One day, some of these scholars say *intercultural communicative competence*, another *democratic competence*. While most fields of research have done away with the concept of culture for example, many of the 'gurus' from the field still retain the concept (even when they talk about 'democratic culture') instead of introducing important discussions around inequality, racism, injustice or violence. *While reading a given scholar, it is important to become aware of their politico-economic and ideological moorings (e.g. the Left/Right/Centre; affiliations to NGOs; the freemasonry).*

When acquainting ourselves with other types of literature (be they from another field of research or from another part of the world), it is important to approach them from a 'similar-different' perspective so that we don't fall into the trap of favouring one over the other. For example, the idea of Western vs. Eastern thought does not make sense as these cannot but be caricatures. *When engaging with (new) ideas, we must bear in mind these two poles of the continuum.*

One important thing that I learnt through my engagement with sociology of postmodernity, anthropology of the ordinary and process philosophy is that we must beware of the way we treat discourses. Discourses (e.g. transcriptions of interviews) do not always reflect realities, and vice versa. As intellectuals, we must find ways to deal with and be transparent about these contradictions. I don't mean here that we should find some 'Truth' but to indicate linguistically that we are aware of repositionings of our research participants so we don't seem to be accusing them of something or convincing our readers that this is the 'Truth'. *It is thus important that scholars are reflexive about their influences on what people do and say and include it in their work. Usually what people say and do in contexts of research relies on what we ask them to say and perform.*

Finally, we need spaces for constructive disagreement in the field of interculturality. The more we read, the more we can learn to do this by including diverse ways of thinking. The field of interculturality is somewhat centered around a few gurus around the world at the moment who rarely talk to each other. *We need clashes of ideologies to happen, especially if they can help us move forward in the field and be more relevant for today's 'intercultural issues'. We need people to come clean about their ideologies, their (hidden) agendas (promotion, advertising for their research group, etc.) and the economic-political forces that support and spread their work. I also believe that a clash of ideologies could empower other (somewhat silenced) ideologies to emerge.*

## (A.S.)

> Modern consciousness is possessed with the idea of "scientific philosophy",
> it is hypnotized by the idea of the scientific. But there is nothing really new:
> it is only the modernised expression of the old scholastic idea.
>
> (Berdyaev, 1962: 23)

## Problems about research on interculturality

At the end of the previous chapter, I argued that here is an urgent need to ethically grapple with interculturality in this time of coronavirus and beyond. If we think about the biopolitics of interculturality, these apparatuses have been produced and reproduced time and time again. Research, and researchers, have certainly played an active and important role. Today I am no longer surprised when either reviewing or reading publications about interculturality, which continually reproduce culturalist prejudices and biases. Culturalism functions as a *de facto* form of racism in the biopolitical apparatus. Research, and researchers themselves (I do not differentiate between research and researchers because I see research as an ethical act of the person), have directly contributed to the ordering and structuring of biopolitical forces within societies. Research and researchers about interculturality often 'box in' their subjects – whether theoretically, logically, methodologically or analytically. As such, there is an inherent incommensurability: there is no common standard and no way of comparing subjects, contexts and environments in research on interculturality. Yet often, researchers often feel the need to compare x to y (whether concepts, notions or people) about interculturality. There is another problem at the heart of this problematique: the obsession with comparing actually reinforces separation and distancing, the other becomes an even further referential object. To put this another way, research about interculturality reproduces a biopolitical ghettoisation (the reproduction of ghettos) by the 'boxing in' of research subjects and their contexts/ environments whereby the research participants remain marginal (especially when the researcher believes they are giving 'agency', 'voice' and 'power' to their research participants). We have all fallen into this at one time or another: *the other is other and always remains other.* For example, I have seen, and reviewed, so much research about 'migrants' and 'refugees' which falls into the biopolitical doctrine of reproducing cultural differences: keeping 'them' politically and socially marginalised as per the doctrine of modernity. This 'life' has been reproduced time and time again by both researchers who reproduce neoracism and ethnocentrism to liberal researchers who rationalise cultural differences. This rationalisation also extends to linguistic and language differences: culture and language are both biopolitical constructs insofar they both conform life to the political (forces of 'us' versus 'them').

For Berdyaev,

> Rationalism is something different from an abstraction of reason from the whole man [*sic*], from humanity, and therefore it is anti-human even if at times it seeks to enter the lists on behalf of the liberation of [*sic*] man.
>
> (Berdyaev, 1962: 22)

This is one of the seductive images of the *simulacrum of the liberal interculturalist*: the compassionate and caring self who respects and tolerates the other, who believes they are empowering the other from their subjugation. The paradox lies in the fact that the rationalising process (the separation of mind from body) engenders superiority and inferiority. When one thinks about how cultural differences have been rationalised through research on interculturality for decades, Esposito argues,

> culture de-solidarizes, if it erects barriers and constructs genres, if it defines gradations in the participation in the notion of humanity, tracing horrible borders between "us" and the "barbarians".
>
> (Esposito, 2020)

For Esposito, culture de-solidarises, it is an extension of biopolitical life: it continues the separation of 'us' and 'them'. At this stage, I need to be honest to the reader that I have purposely not included the final line of this quote from Esposito. This is due to the fact one needs to arrive through a full deconstruction of interculturality in the subsequent subsections to come. I will problematise the final line of Esposito's quotation in the final remarks of this chapter. The point I am trying to make here is that this chapter started with the question: *What's good and bad about research on interculturality today?* The question itself is perhaps not adequate to what I am arguing for (the binary toing and froing is not sufficient), which is the destabilisation and dismantling of research about interculturality in order to move beyond biopolitical *dispositifs* and simulacra about how research on interculturality has contributed to the ordering of sociopolitical life.

In the quote from Berdyaev at the beginning of this section, he argues something which often resonates with me when researching and teaching interculturality: the obsession with the 'scientific', or how researchers are hypnotised by the scientific in their own work. I have often been amazed and shocked at how researchers continually shift and jump at gurus, 'fashionable' concepts and/or 'fashionable' approaches and theories in scholarly work on interculturality. The second part of this quote also resonates another point: the reinvention of scientific wheels, whereby the old is masquerading as new 'knowledge'. This is something which Fred and I have spoken about year after year. Part of me wants to believe that research and teaching about interculturality has reached an impasse, whereby scholars and teachers are looking for new inspirations and angles in their work. This may or may not be true. But the cynic in me actually believes that this constant reproduction of "reinventing the same wheels" about interculturality time and time again relates to how the field functions as a biopolitical apparatus *par excellence*: through focusing on culturalism, it preserves and orders the structuration of life as being constituted through 'us' versus 'them'. Focusing on 'culture' and 'cultural differences' engenders the separation needed to control populations within a given context (e.g. by describing what values/notions/behaviour can be considered as being from context *x's* 'culture', they automatically demarcate them from what they are not). Research, and researchers, who reproduce these logics and practices in their work are actively contributing to this biopolitical apparatus. The question then lies in terms of how one can depart the biopolitical apparatus or whether one can depart these processes and logics at all.

## Research on interculturality has taken self-identity as truth: a liberal critique

One of the ways I propose in rethinking some of the issues about how (and why) one carries out research on interculturality lies in how one thinks about 'truth' and how the notion of truth is constructed. Going back to the quotation from Berdyaev at the beginning, research about interculturality should involve questioning the idea of the scientific knowledge and truth, and importantly, one's being in relation to these notions. The Russian word *istina* [истина], unlike its French translation *vérité*, has a primarily ontological sense: it means: "what is, what truly exists". This is due to the fact that 'truth', *istina*, is linguistically close to the verb 'to be': *istina-estina*. For centuries, there have been philosophical disagreements over the meaning of *istina* as true (ontological) existence and *istina* as true (epistemological) judgement (e.g. statements conforming to a given reality). In a sense, *istinia* etymologically can be used in both ways.

For the Russian philosopher Vladimir Solovyov (1853–1900), "what truth (*istina*) is, one must at least say what it is not. It is not in the realm of the separate and isolated self" (Solovyov, 1965: 213). For Solovyov, a 19th-century rationalist philosopher, *istina* is thus the self-identify of the supra-personal objective world; it is revealed to the mind that thinks itself. This interpretation of *istina* (truth) resonates to me the ways in which liberal interculturalists have proclaimed 'truths' in the field. The problem with self-identity is a human being never coincides with himself. The formula of identity "A is A" is not applicable to him (Sidorkin, 1999; Simpson, 2018; Simpson and Dervin, 2019b). For Mikhail Bakhtin, the basis of being human (or human being) is not self-identity but the opening of dialogue, an opening which always implies the simultaneous inter-animation of more than one voice (Sidorkin, 1999). In this sense, s/he may say they are gay or lesbian or bisexual, speak multiple languages, have multiple identities, and multiple languages (which may or may not be true), but whether these things are true or not is not the point Bakhtin is making here – these aspects of our being, and becoming, are constantly co-constructed as acts of co-being as they are always produced by and with others. Because human beings are social beings, we always action our existence with others and through others.

The overly simplistic statements that one hears, such as "the person is British therefore they identify to British culture", or "French is my culture because French is my mother tongue language" are rendered obsolete. When self-identity is conceptualised as rationalised truth, it objectifies the person. The essence of the person becomes generalised because the mind (superior) is separated from the body (inferior). The body becomes a slave to phantasm of the mind and truth (*istina*) becomes a phantasm of the mind. This process can lead to essentialisms and stereotypes through generalisations about the self: the mind creates certain images about itself, yet there is no way of knowing if they are true because they cannot be contested (because rationalists believe the mind is superior). In this sense, self-identity can produce dogmas about people and about notions as the person and concepts are conceptualised normatively, rather than thinking about people and concept as being dynamically constructed.

Alternatively, for Nikolai Berdyaev who views *istina* (truth) and being from an ontological and dynamic perspective:

> I am the way, the truth (*istina*) and the life. What does this phrase mean? It means that truth (*istina*) is not intellectual or exclusively gnoseological [philosophy of knowledge or theory of knowledge] in character, but that it has to be understood comprehensively: it is existential.
>
> (Berdyaev, 1962: 21)

Berdyaev argues, "truth is communitarian (istina kommjunotarna [истина коммюнотарна]); in other words, it assumes contact (soobščenie [сообщение] and fraternity between [*sic*] men" (Ibid.). Here, *soobščenie* means communion. For Berdyaev, it is freedom *svoboda* that gives an absolute character to human subjectivity. "But human creation always implies a departure from self, an elimination of self, and is only realized in the communion with others" (Vasylchenko (2014: 514). In this sense, truth (*istinia*) cannot be actualised in an objective sense that is independent or above relations between human beings. *Istina*, which is thus dynamic in essence, is multidirectional as it refers to intersubjectivities: for Berdyaev, it is the aggregate of these intersubjectivities which constitutes truth (*istina*).

## A way forward for interculturality: rethinking the ground between istina (truth) and postupok (the ethical act)

In contrast to Berdyaev, Mikhail Bakhtin, instead, contrasts *istina* to *Pravda (truth in justice)*. For Bakhtin, the (ethical) act is unable to contain *postupok* – the subject is no longer the knowing subject but the acting subject. In this sense, *istina* "retains its epistemological meaning, 'what is, from the objective or scientific point of view,' but it is relieved of its ontological meaning: it can no longer refer to 'what truly exists'" (Vasylchenko (2014: 515).

For Bakhtin,

> "What truly exists" is not *istina*, but *postupok*, an act invested with *pravda*. The world of "what is," within which *postupok* takes place, is the being-event (*bytie-sobytie*). With this term Bakhtin introduces an ctymological metaphor: *sobytie* means "event," but literally *so-bytie* signifies "co-being" [and] "co-existence".
>
> (Vasylchenko (2014: 515)

From the discussions in earlier chapters, I introduced the Bakhtinian notion of *there is no alibi in being*. This notion is central to Bakhtin's work. Bakhtin discusses *istina* (truth) as *postupok* (ethical act) because "Being is Being" for Bakhtin. The person is present in the moment, in the act. The person exists authentically – there is no transfiguration of the self. It is *postupok* (the ethical act) whereby truth is co-constructed, negotiated and actioned by interlocutors in a dialogue. The interlocutors in these dialogues co-construct, negotiate and perform their own being as co-being (*so-bytie*), with and through others. Therefore, *istina* is not necessarily an ontological question for Bakhtin because one *is* (i.e. the person is before your eyes co-constructing the event with you; therefore, the person exists). For research on interculturality, my argument is that there are merits in finding a convergence between Bakhtin and Berdyaev insofar as it is important to recognise the co-acts, co-events that one participates in research and in social life – these acts demand our ethical questioning and problematisation. This is particularly important for researchers who should be reflexive about all of the aspects contained within their research and teaching on interculturality (from the notions and concepts, definitions, methodologies and analyses, to the participants in the work and the researchers' own influences, stances, ideologies and utterances).

I would agree with Bakhtin that *there is no alibi in being*; therefore, being is constructed as co-events (*bytie-sobytie*) with the other, but this is also an ontological question which lies in the relationality between the self and the other. The fact that a crisis of outsideness exists between the self and the other, meaning no stable or evaluative position can be maintained, means that the self and other are in a perpetual position of constantly questioning the essence of themselves and the other. I propose understanding the relationship between *istina* (truth) and *postupok* (the ethical act) as a continuum, a constant back and forth movement within the self and between the self and the other. Additionally, it is important to use the relationship between *istina* and *postupok* in order to question the realities of 'scientific knowledge' (so they do not turn into dogmas and norms) – therefore, I take up a position in between Bakhtin and Berdyaev insofar that *istina* should be used to provoke questions about the realms and limits of what can be considered as 'truth' and/or 'knowledge'. In this sense, *istina* is both epistemological and ontological.

In Figure 5.1, I have modified the figure from Chapter 2 to demonstrate the following way to problematise interculturality:

*Figure 5.1* Figure 1.2 revisited (an alternative sense of interculturality)

*Istina* is now included as one of the main notions at the heart of rethinking interculturality. *Istina* retains its epistemological meaning. The notion questions the foundation of knowledge. This is particularly important for teaching and scholarship on interculturality with reference to the biopolitical schemas and apparatuses at the heart of conservative and liberal approaches to interculturality, who must be countered.

The being of interculturality is always in the making – meaning it is always in the becoming. This is important for researchers and teachers to reflect upon, that knowledge is never fixed at and end point with regard to interculturality. It is always in the making. Thus, no one can ever have complete knowledge about what interculturality is, today or tomorrow. It is important not to fall into the trap of impotent criticality – towards translations, definitions, notions, concepts, meanings, approaches and methodologies used in research on interculturality.

Perhaps within the question of what is good about research on interculturality is the question: What should inspire research on interculturality? Knowledge should be co-constructed, co-created as co-events (*bytie-sobytie*) of being, which should aim to find commonalities and differences whilst destabilising and decentring normative dogmas. It is necessary and important for scholarship and teaching on interculturality to reject and abandon the reinvention of biopolitical intercultural wheels, which I have demonstrated in this chapter and the previous chapter. Critical interculturality rejects the biopolitics of conservative and liberal interculturalists. I have proposed a figure in this chapter to move beyond these logics and practices. Research on interculturality should always problematise the following questions: For whom? By whom? For what purpose?

Perhaps there is also a question contained within the question of what is bad about research on interculturality: What should research on interculturality be about?

Research on interculturality could include aspects such as problematising fears/anxieties (about death, the other, mental health issues, economic insecurity, being, identities, relationships with people and systems) as a basis of commonality and difference (not just simply focusing on differences). This will allow interculturality to focus on problematising what unites us (in co-existence with other human beings). This involves questioning the essence of commonalities we all share/experience and live through, all of these aspects throughout our lives wherever we live, wherever we migrate to, wherever we were born, the languages we speak, the identities we have, the pain, suffering and everything in between – this is what unites our co-being and co-existence; not 'culture' or 'cultural differences'.

## Final remarks

The question of whether research on interculturality is good or bad is ultimately an ethical question. This relates to understanding research on interculturality as an ethical act in itself. This is due to the fact of the inherent epistemological and ontological etymology of the word *istina* and its relation to *postupok*. By ethical, I mean non-normative dialogical ethics which I have proposed as a way forward for research on interculturality.

Earlier in this chapter, I said I decided not to include the final line of Esposito's quotation on the current coronavirus pandemic. Here is the quotation in full:

> culture de-solidarizes, if it erects barriers and constructs genres, if it defines gradations in the participation in the notion of humanity, tracing horrible borders between "us" and the "barbarians", the virus connects, and forces us to search for common solutions.
>
> (Esposito, 2020)

In the final line of this quote, Esposito argues that in this current time of coronavirus, the virus can help reconnect humanity. Critical interculturality must be about finding the ways and means of reconnecting humanity today and tomorrow. Through the figure, I have proposed that co-being and co-existence through non-normative dialogical ethics could be a site to rework and reconnect these aspects. In previous publications, Fred and I (Simpson and Dervin, 2019b) have proposed intercultural co-competencies based upon non-normative dialogical ethics to incorporate co-being and dialogism into scholarship on interculturality. At the same time, critical interculturality must reject and abandon the conservative and liberal biopolitics of interculturality. On the social and animal characteristics of human beings, Berdyaev sums this point up well:

> The animal nature of man [*sic*], and indeed his social nature too, is objectification and alienation rather than *Existenz* which is revealed only in subjectivity and individuality. Man [*sic*] as an animal is an object, that is to say something which is different from and opposed to the depth of his existence.
>
> (Berdyaev, 1962: 17)

As I have argued consistently throughout this chapter and the previous chapter, the ethical act *postupok* for interculturality research (and researchers) lies in rejecting the notions, concepts, definitions, approaches and methods of conservative and liberal biopolitical approaches to interculturality. The ethical act lies in the fact there is *no alibi in interculturality* because there *is no alibi in being*.

## [Synopsis]

Intercultural research is global, wide-ranging and encompasses different subfields. Yet its globality is dominated by a limited amount of privileged voices, mostly from Western English-speaking scholars. What is more, like all other research fields, it is embedded in the global corporate identity of today's academia, which means that it is a product that is sold to educators, businessmen, governments and supranational institutions. Economic-political forces have an influence on what the field researches, what it publishes, and where and who it influences.

We both listed a long list of problems with the field:

- Research on interculturality contributes to ordering and structuring bio-political forces within societies. The knowledge that it constructs is presented as the only (acceptable) 'Truth' about the notion.
- There are artificial boundaries between the different fields of research that work on intercultural issues, which limits interdisciplinary cooperation and dialogue. The concepts used in the field tend to be used when they become fashionable. Often, they represent mere impoverished anachronic versions of concepts from other fields.
- Intercultural research can too easily perform 'false generosity' by ordering people to 'respect each other', 'be tolerant', 'live democratically!', etc.
- The aforementioned privileged voices are hardly ever questioned. They tend to be 'recycled' and spread around the globe. *Their interculturality becomes everybody's interculturality – even if it does not correspond to 'our' reality*!
- Research methods and analytical frameworks used in the field are still too monological and ignore the inevitable hyphen between self and the Other – no self without the Other and vice versa. Although critical perspectives on interculturality place *identity as co-construction* at the centre of analysis, the way data are analysed still focuses on the individual, as if they were separated from other individuals.
- The way researchers talk about interculturality 'over' those they represent in their research – in the sense that they construct research participants' realities – often imposes interpretations and essentialist visions of the Other's experience. If those represented have access to the research written about them, they could experience it as microaggressions.

In the chapter, we also made some suggestions to make a difference in terms of how intercultural research is done. The overarching idea that ethics should be central to research on interculturality was emphasised.

## [Going further]

Now consider the following questions:

- Who are the most important scholars in the field of interculturality for you? What do you know about them?

- Have you read a book, an article or heard a talk about interculturality from a scholar who is not from the 'West'? What did you learn from them? What would you like to know more about their ideas?
- Can you read research in different languages? How much does multilingual engagement with research help develop polycentric ideas about interculturality? Are you aware of any potential influence of this aspect on how you see interculturality in education research?
- Do you have a pet theory or a concept that you like? Explain why.
- What about theories or concepts that you disagree with (or feel indifferent to)?
- What is the most convincing critique of a mainstream theory or concept of which you are aware?
- Have you ever collected research data in relation to interculturality? What ethical problems did you encounter? For example, did you feel you were able to be faithful to the way your research participants were constructing their realities?
- Finally, what do you think should be done globally to counter the dominance of 'Western' voices in the field of interculturality?

## Note

1 See e.g. Qu Weiguo (2020).

# 6    The intercultural is always ideological and political

> You can't discuss the ocean with a well-frog, he's limited to the space he lives in. You can't discuss ice with a summer insect – he's bound to a single season.
>
> Zhuangzi, The Complete Works of Chuang Tzu

This last chapter illustrates the concrete politics of interculturality in the form of a response to a response to one of our publications in the journal *Intercultural Communication Education* (Publisher: Castledown). Our article is entitled "The Council of Europe Reference Framework of Competences for Democratic Culture: Ideological refractions, othering and obedient politics" (Simpson & Dervin, 2019) and is summarised as follows:

> The popularity of the idea of interculturality, in different parts of the world, means that there are many differing meanings and ways in which the notion is understood, represented, and expressed. In contrast to the polysemy of the intercultural, democracy often appears on the surface to be understood through universalist and/or absolutist conceptualisations. Combining the intercultural and democracy thus requires problematisation. In this article we use *The Council of Europe Reference Framework on Competencies for Democratic Culture* (2018) as an example showing how the notion of the intercultural is constructed. We use a form of intertextuality in order to show the performance of competing ideologies found in this document. Some of the ideologies found within the texts clearly mark Eurocentric discourses and a stigmatisation of the other. Also, the way in which the political is sanitised can engender a language of depoliticisation and obedience. As a result, we problematise *Critical Interculturality* as a way to move beyond culturalist self-centered notions of the intercultural arguing that the political and the social cannot be separated from the intercultural when discussing democracy.

In August 2020, Barrett and Byram wrote a response to our paper entitled "Errors by Simpson and Dervin (2019) in their description of the Council of Europe's Reference Framework of Competences for Democratic Culture". In what follows, we respond to Barrett & Byram and reaffirm the main arguments of our paper on *The Council of Europe's Reference Framework of Competencies for Democratic Culture* (RFCDC) (2019a). What follows summarises many of the points that were made in the previous chapters and thus serves as a case study of the politics of interculturality in research. We encourage the reader to read the Council of Europe experts' response.

Responding to a response emerging from experts is an important task for intellectuals, and when it comes to issues of interculturality, a highly political and ideological problematic, responses which might lead to change, epistemological justice and transparency should be never-ending. It will be obvious to the reader of both our original paper and the experts' response that our political and ideological perspectives differ entirely. Thus, we do not expect to enter into a dialogue and/or convince them that our views are also 'correct' or 'accurate' (to use modernist terms like the word 'errors' used by them in their response), but we see this response as an important warning to those working with issues of interculturality and democracy. Our presupposition and starting point are transparent: *the intercultural is always ideological and political*. The content of Barrett & Byram's response and of our own response to their response make no exception to the rule.

Both of our papers on the RFCDC (2019a; 2019b) are rigorous scientific efforts to open up and contest the purpose, aims, meanings and implications of such a comprehensive instrument. Having noticed the potential danger that such frameworks/models represent when used without being problematised, critiqued and/or modified in e.g. China and Finland, our papers were written to help other scholars and practitioners be aware of, identify and reject (should need be) some of their hidden meanings and agendas. As we have argued many times in the previous chapters, one should always bear in mind that such models/frameworks are produced for supranational institutions which are first and foremost political entities, projecting specific ideologies.

Before we reaffirm succinct implications for the reader to take away and use from our research, one important point needs to be made about their response to our research article: Barrett and Byram seem to deny the role of ideology in the RFCDC. Valentin Volosinov shows how ideology functions succinctly: "in actual fact, each living ideological sign has two faces, like Janus. Any current curse word can become a word of praise, any current truth must inevitably sound to many other people as the greatest lie" (Volosinov, 1973: 23). Or, to quote Althusser (2001: 108): "Ideology never says 'I am ideological'". This is manifested in the following features of their response: **1)** Why is it that Barrett & Byram fail to state that they are acknowledged by The Council of Europe as part of the authoring team of the project in the body of the paper? This information is stated explicitly on p. 9 in each of the three volumes that make up the RFCDC (Council of Europe, 2018a; 2018b; 2018c). In their response, why do they not inform the reader of their roles and responsibilities in producing the three volumes and about any partiality they might have towards the RFCDC project? Barrett and Byram's response assumes that the reader is naïve to the role they played in producing the three volumes of the RFCDC, and their statements about "factual errors", "interpretative errors" and "category errors" attempt to further perpetuate the view that the RFCDC is an ideologically neutral document that can only be interpreted 'accurately' or 'inaccurately'. This is clearly insufficient – one must remember that "wherever a sign is present, ideology is present, too" (Volosinov, 1973: 10) **2)** They authored the three volumes along with 11 other experts. We would have expected more of the original diverse team (in terms of gender, ethnicity, race, language, status, social class, etc.) to have been involved in responding to our paper. Such lack of diverse voices and acknowledgment seems to obscure the position(s) the two authors are taking in their response: scholars and/or practitioners and/or potential project leaders (?) and/or experts promoting the work of the Council of Europe. In other words, whose voice(s) are we hearing in the response? **3)** This last point is essential: Not only are these experts failing to disclose the practical roles and responsibilities they played in the project but also the fact that these roles and responsibilities are political as the Council of Europe is a political organisation. The lack of criticality and self-reflexivity shown by these experts about their own biases and ideologies represents precisely the same mantra of insisting ideological neutrality and, at the same time, ideological impositions that we have deconstructed in our research on the RFCDC.

Reading through Barrett & Byram's response, we felt that dialogue is impossible. Like Zhuangzi elaborates, we end up discussing the ocean with a well-frog. We have already proposed a critical and ontological approach to the intercultural through dialogical ethics (Simpson & Dervin, 2019b; 2019c; 2019d). Similarly, we propose the following ways to move beyond Barrett and Byram's mantras:

1   The RFCDC is not sacred writ. The current multiplication of Eurocentric/modernist models of intercultural competence, global competence (e.g. the OECD PISA Global Competence) and democratic competence, often disguised as international models, means there is a constant need to cross-examine the polysemy and economic-political agendas of these initiatives.

2   Intercultural dogmas must be deconstructed. Here, the focus should be on unpacking and contesting concepts, relations and positions rather than falling into the trap of assumptions and generalisations about how things *are* or how they *ought* to be.

3   The political and the economic cannot be separated from the cultural. Culture does not exist as such. It has no agency; it is not palpable. One cannot meet a culture but people who (are made to) represent it – or rather represent imaginaries and representations of it (Dervin, 2016). Thus, every social order is a contingent articulation of power relations that lacks an ultimate rational ground meaning that every social order is political and economic. These notions are irreducible to one another, yet they are mutually inseparable from each other.

4   Universalist approaches to democracy, human rights and the intercultural are impotent. As Esposito argues (2008: xvii): "The autoimmune topology always dictates that democracy [human rights and the intercultural] be sent off [*renvoyer*] elsewhere, that it be excluded or rejected, expelled under pretext of protecting it on the inside by expelling, rejecting, or sending off to the outside". The inherent inescapability of exclusion becomes the paradox of universalism.

5   The hidden political and economic influences on intercultural research must always be questioned. Questioning the social, political and economic voices (and actors!) should be part of intercultural research. The point of our research is to warn our readers about the hidden meanings of the Framework and the need to be trained to unearth the ideologies that lie behind. All models of intercultural competence also need to be examined critically.

The desire and need for 'real' intercultural dialogue in research and practice is arguably required now more than ever. But is it possible? The 2020 COVID-19 crisis has removed the intercultural veil over some sections of society and revealed prevalent forms of injustice, xenophobia and racism (ills that we were well aware of before). Xenophobia and racism have been in society throughout human history, yet, often regarding global and intercultural competencies, we hear that one needs to be *more respectful, more tolerant, more open towards the other.* Why? To masquerade the self as being open, tolerant and respectful when one potentially may hold racist and xenophobic views? The challenge posed by post-COVID-19 is to not fall into the trap and be seduced by Eurocentric/modernist models about global/intercultural/democratic competencies anymore. What the COVID-19 crisis has demonstrated is that many of the intercultural ideologies that the world has been fed over the past 70 years might have failed to help us (amongst others): 1. see beyond our own imaginaries (*"we have 'democracy', they don't*"), 2. rid us of ethnocentrism ("*in our culture we care about 'individuals', they don't*") and 3. be more 'critically critical' ("*their media are brainwashing them, ours are correct and objective*") (see Dervin et al., 2020). By focusing exclusively on culture, language and communication (amongst others), these intercultural ideologies might have blinded us and made us forget about the major influences of neoliberal politics and the economy on our encounters. This is why we need to continually problematise the relevance and purpose of models like the RFCDC through 'digging' into the multiplicity of ideologies that construct the concepts and notions, allowing us to escape from specific dogmas and impositions through proposing counter-narratives and counter-practices – again and again.

Finally, in order to get a full sense of our endeavour, the reader might wish to get acquainted with our companion papers on the RFCDC (Simpson & Dervin, 2019b) and on the OECD's global and intercultural competencies (Simpson & Dervin, 2019c).

## [Synopsis]

Criticality and reflexivity are two central strategies to adopt when researching and educating for interculturality. An assertion about interculturality is never neutral and is always influenced not only by our own beliefs, experiences and political thoughts but also by education and state apparatuses (amongst others). When acquainting ourselves with a document (e.g. a Reference Framework) supported by a supranational institution with specific worldviews, it is important that we evaluate the 'invisible' orders given by its authors and the ideologies that go with them. Political and economic pressure on the production of such frameworks must also be examined critically.

## [Going further]

Acquaint yourself with *The Council of Europe's Reference Framework of Competencies for Democratic Culture* (RFCDC): www.coe.int/en/web/education/competences-for-democratic-culture (Who wrote it? Why? Who sponsored it? Etc.). Then read the original article that we published in 2019 (Simpson & Dervin, 2019a) as well as the response published by Barrett & Byram (2020). And then try to answer the following questions:

- What are your impressions of the Reference Framework? Who do you think it can benefit? What problems do you see in using it (for example, outside Europe, where it has already been promoted)?
- Are there elements in our original article and in the response with which you agree/disagree or are not sure about?

- Going back to the previous chapters, are you able to identify some of the problems that we have discussed in the Reference Framework? For example: *Who is talking for whom in the three volumes?*
- What do you make of the following comments introduced in this chapter?

  - "One should always bear in mind that such models/frameworks are produced for supranational institutions which are first and foremost political entities, projecting specific ideologies",
  - "The RFCDC is not sacred writ".
  - "The focus should be on unpacking and contesting concepts, relations and positions rather than falling into the trap of assumptions and generalisations about how things *are* or how they *ought* to be".
  - "Universalist approaches to democracy, human rights and the intercultural are impotent".

# Conclusion

For the French writer G. Flaubert (1989: xxxvii), "Stupidity lies in wanting to draw conclusions". Thinking of our discussions in this book, it would be pretentious (and stupid?) to draw 'final' conclusions on the notion of interculturality. A lot remains to be done to continue to unearth the complexities of interculturality. We maintain that research and education have only scratched its surface until now, often contributing to making it look like a fetish with magical powers.

Our book represents an attempt to provide some answers to five important questions about this thorny notion:

- *What to make of the notion of interculturality?*
- *Who was influential in the ways we understand interculturality?*
- *How does intercultural research and education influence experiences of interculturality?*
- *Can we prepare/get prepared for interculturality?*
- *What is the state of research on interculturality today?*

While engaging with these questions, we emphasised the importance to be systematically critical and reflexive about what we have to say about interculturality. We had both similarities and differences in the way we see the notion today and the way it is being dealt with in research and education. Our answers not only should be seen as 'red flags' but also as an invitation to meaningful, critical and reflexive dialogues – instead of muting certain aspects of the conversation about interculturality. A prevailing theme throughout the book was to look into interculturality through the lenses of ideologies and of the economic-political. This can allow us to "hold the ship out beyond that surf and spray" (Aristotle in Ackrill, 1987: 386). Dealing with interculturality does not follow a straight-line method.

**What to take away from this book?**

In what follows, we have summarised the main points to take away from the book. Recommendations and principles are proposed. We only cover three aspects of interculturality in education: 1. *Conceptualising*, 2. *Researching* and 3. *Preparing*. We have consciously excluded recommendations and/ or principles for encountering the Other since we believe that this part of interculturality is not up to researchers and/or educators to decide what these should be about and how they should take place. Another book is needed to dig deeper into this aspect.

## 1 Conceptualising

**Recommendations**

- Do a background check of the knowledge you wish to use:

  - Do the archeology of the chosen knowledge in different fields and contexts in as many languages as possible

    - About the scholars you refer to: ask the question of "which interculturality are they?"
    - Identify any economic-political affiliation, supranational sponsoring or tribes and reflect on the consequences on the way these scholars conceptualise interculturality and other concepts/notions
    - When combining scholars: Do their ideologies match? What potential contradictions?

- Critique unquestioned and widely accepted ideas, concepts and notions. Never satisfy yourself with the 'normal'.
- Trace meanings and 'travel' of concepts, notions, theories and ideologies in different languages (translation, etymology, polysemy, etc.).
- Identify less-known ideas, especially from other fields of knowledge and different parts of the world. Systematically promote less heard voices of scholars, writers, artists, etc.

**Principles for conceptualising from a critical interculturality perspective**

- No one can ever 'master' interculturality because 'mastering' interculturality would mean mastering *being* – a being in the singular which would reflect a totalised 'end', i.e. the idea that the self can acquire a certain intercultural essence – certain attributes/skills/competencies in order to perform interculturality and/or or *be* 'intercultural'. There will never be any real way of knowing whether the self actually believes in, or understands anything about, the notions and skills which are often attributed to interculturality such as *tolerance* and *respect*: therefore, interculturality cannot be vested in, or treated as, mere lip service for mimicry and masquerade.

- Critical interculturality rejects the seduction of the simulacrum of the liberal interculturalist: interculturality needs to be decentred away from images of self-centrism and other-centrisms. This point relates to the liberalist political grammar of interculturality which focuses on (implicitly and explicitly) modifying/changing/adapting the self and/or the other within the wider functioning sociopolitical *dispositif* (apparatus).
- Critical interculturality acknowledges that a sociopolitical consensus cannot be reached about either the political or interculturality: this entails rejecting ethico-political dogmas about how interculturality is or how it ought to be whilst recognising the inherently conflictual characteristics of societies and human beings.
- However, it is important that by focusing on the inherently conflictual nature of societies that structures of domination are not reproduced or normalised (like liberal intercultural approaches). For critical interculturality, this involves moving beyond universalism, universalism about human beings, universalism about definitions and concepts, universalism about values and notions and so forth. The paradox of universalism lies not only in the impotence of its unequal distribution and application but also in its normative ideological function. Under liberal universalism, values and notions turn into dogmas and ethico-political judgement criteria and impositions which negate the principles of freedom and diversity upon which universalism is supposed to be founded.
- Critical interculturality rejects the biopolitics of interculturality: the rationalisation of racism without race discourses and the rationalisation of differentialist biases about cultural differences and culture. The project of liberalism continued the separation of man [sic] and animal through rationalism – the mind became superior to the inferior body. In liberal interculturalist terms this lineage was continued through rationalising cultural differences. Like races previous who needed to become 'more civilised', 'more democratic' and 'more open', in more recent years the semantic shift has been to cultures who need to be 'more civilised', 'more democratic' and 'more open'. The political grammar of culture and cultural difference discourses today demarcates the lexicon of how the superior and the inferior are understood.

• Instead, critical interculturality could be problematised from a non-normative dialogical perspective which aims for the continuous problematisation of ideas, notions and beings. This means rejecting certain notions (e.g. culture, respect, tolerance). If culture desolidarises (it engenders an 'us' versus 'them'), then critical interculturality involves finding out what solidarises.

## 2 Researching

### Recommendations

• Weight the pros and cons of a specific theory, concept, method, etc. and be transparent about them.
• Don't fall into the trap of 'fashionable' research terms and methods. An archeology of these is also needed.
• Feel free to reject certain ideologies about how to 'do' research and education on interculturality. Be clear as to why.
• Be vigilant and skeptical when choosing a research topic and research participants. Try not to 'mistreat' your research participants by judging them implicitly/explicitly.
• Put yourself in your research:

   • What is your potential influence and that of others on what you are researching?
   • What is your starting point? Are your political, economic and associational affiliations influencing your research on interculturality?
   • How does your own experience of interculturality impact on what you are researching and writing about?

### Principles for researching from a critical interculturality perspective

• Research about the intercultural is always ideological and political.
• Truth and knowledge about critical interculturality should always be continuously problematised. This movement involves putting oneself within the research process in terms of how truth and knowledge are constructed – this movement is both ontological and epistemological. It involves questioning how we understand our (social, political, economic) relationships to the concepts, notions and methods we use. This process is inherently reflexive and critical as it also involves questioning both I and others in the research process (e.g. when selecting, analysing and collecting data from research participants).

- Critical interculturality involves mapping the archaeology and etymology of notions, definitions and concepts used in research. Often, there are multiple words in one language to reflect one English word in intercultural research yet often researchers exclusively and solely use that particular one English word. This is problematic as researchers often use the English equivalent words without addressing the sociopolitical and linguistic archaeology of what the word means and especially when the word reflects an ideological position. Researchers must also 'dig' into and problematise the polysemy of words (concepts, definitions, notions) used in research on interculturality.
- Reject limiting and/or limited approaches about interculturality. Instead of reinventing the liberal intercultural wheel over and over again, critical interculturality demands multidirectional thinking about notions, concepts and theories which can influence and inspire future research. Too often researchers 'play safe' by reproducing a model from a white English-speaking 'guru' on interculturality rather than looking for inspiration and knowledge from different (e.g. local, regional, linguistic) disciplines or fields. Researchers should:

  1 Refrain from falling into the trap of methodological nationalism whereby they concentrate on representatives of one country rather than looking at experiences with people from other contexts.
  2 Researchers need to be aware of how their own research can reproduce political, social and economic forms of symbolic violence by the decisions they make in their research on interculturality (e.g. the definitions, concepts, approaches they use). Symbolic violence is reproduced when one group becomes dominated, excluded or prejudiced against by another – symbolic violence functions through naturalising or universalising power relations through commonsensical ways of thinking and speaking.

## 3 Preparing

### Recommendations

- Unprepare to (be) prepare(d):
  - Consider your own past acts of sociality to be *already* acts of interculturality from which you may find some inspiration.
  - Question 'invisible' orders and intercultural intimidation (e.g. "Be tolerant!", "Promote European identity!"). It might hurt to step out of these orders and to face different realities, but it is increasingly necessary to liberate oneself from them.

- Reverse the tendency to copy 'good practices'.
- Consider misunderstandings and non-understandings as learning moments.
- Question 'techniques' against the potential imposition of world-views onto the other (e.g. 'democratic culture').
- Privilege spontaneity over calculation ("Go with the flow").
- Accept that we will never get close enough to the other – any kind of other.

**Principles for preparing from a critical interculturality perspective**

- The moments, experiences and encounters in interculturality (and in life generally speaking) cannot prepare one to meet the other. The crises of outsideness between the self and other(s) means that no stable evaluative position can ever be maintained between the self and the other(s). One can never know what the other is demanding of them (e.g. what they are thinking, how they will act and behave, how their knowledge and worldviews have been constituted).
- *There is no alibi in interculturality because there is no alibi in being*: one is ultimately obligated, and immediately called, to act ethically. There is no hiding place in interculturality. The emphasis is on understanding why I think, feel, behave and understand in a particular situation and how I have come to think, feel, behave and understand in this way in this situation. There are no 'good' nor 'bad' experiences here, no 'good' nor 'bad' ways to communicate or interact. Instead, the focus is on engaging into a dialogue whereby the self does not violate the other, the self does not violate itself or the other does not violate the self (e.g. generalising or essentialising their identities through prejudicing/assuming how they act or behave or exoticising one another through flattery).
- Interculturality must be decontextualised and recontextualised through dialogical ethics. This involves asking oneself questions such as: *Am I imposing my values/beliefs onto the other? Am I letting the other impose their values/beliefs onto me?*
- Critical interculturality acknowledges the relationship between the self and the other as *self-other*, meaning no one can *do* interculturality without others.
- Critical interculturality is actioned through interlocutors engaging into dialogues which produce co-acts, forms of co-being and co-existence. In the sense that human beings are in constant processes of co-learning with others, co-experiencing with others, co-actioning with others, i.e. constantly belonging through, and with, others.
- Critical interculturality should focus on solidarising interculturality through commonalities and differences (not just differences). This

involves questioning the essence of commonalities we all share/experience and live through, all of the aspects throughout our lives wherever we live, wherever we migrate to, wherever we were born, the languages we speak, our identities, the pain, suffering and everything in between – this is what unites our co-being and co-existence, not 'culture' nor 'cultural differences'.

Borrowing a metaphor that the French philosopher Vladimir Jankélévitch used in his conversations with Béatrice Berlowitz (1978: 23), we could say that what our recommendations and principles underline is that engaging with interculturality resembles the complex, curious and somewhat playful position of a butterfly circling around a flame. Playing with the 'fire' of interculturality should be a humbling position that forces us to stand not too close and not too far from it.

# Bibliography

Ackrill, J. L. (Ed.). (1987). *A new Aristotle reader*. Oxford & Princeton: Princeton University Press.

Aduba, U. (2014). Never thought about changing her Nigerian name. Retrieved from www.colorlines.com/articles/uzo-aduba-never-thought-about-changing-her-nigerian-name

Agamben, G. (2020). Clarifications. Retrieved September 20, 2020 from www.journal-psychoanalysis.eu/coronavirus-and-philosophers/

Althusser, L. (1965). *Pour Marx*. Paris: François Maspero.

Althusser, L. (2001). *Lenin and philosophy and other essays*. New York: Monthly Review Press.

Althusser, L. (2011). *Philosophy and the spontaneous philosophy of the scientists & other essays*. London: Verso.

Althusser, L. (2017). *How to be a Marxist in philosophy*. London: Bloomsbury Academic.

Angermuller, J. (2014). *Poststructuralist discourse analysis: Subjectivity in enunciative pragmatics*. Hampshire: Palgrave Macmillan.

Anholt, S. (2009). *Places: Identity, image and reputation*. Hampshire: Palgrave Macmillan.

Aronczyk, M. (2013). *Branding the nation: The global business of national identity*. Oxford: Oxford University Press.

Bakhtin, M. M. (1981). *The dialogic imagination: Four essays* (ed. M. Holquist, trans. C. Emerson & M. Holquist). Austin: University of Texas Press.

Bakhtin, M. M. (1984). *Problems of Dostoevsky's poetics* (ed. & trans. C. Emerson). Austin: University of Texas Press.

Bakhtin, M. M. (1990). *Art and answerability: Early philosophical essays* (eds. M. Holquist & V. Liapunov). Austin, University of Texas Press.

Bakhtin, M. M. (2012). *Sobranie sochinenij. (T.3). Teoriia romana (1930–1961 gg.)* (eds. S. G. Bocharov & Vadim Valer'janovich Kozhinov). Moskva: Jazyki slavianskikh kul'tur.

Balandier, G. (1980). *Le pouvoir sur scènes*. Paris: Ballard.

Balibar, E. (2005). Difference, otherness, exclusion. *Parallax, 11*(1), 19–34.

Barbot, M., & Dervin, F. (2011). *Rencontres interculturelles et formation dossier*. Éducation permanente.

Barthes, R. (2012). *Travels in China*. Cambridge: Polity Press.

Bauman, Z. (1997). *Postmodernity and its discontents*. London: Polity Press.

Bauman, Z. (2004). *Identity: Conversations with Benedetto Vecchi*. Cambridge: Polity Press.

Baumann, G. (1996). *Contesting culture: Discourses of identity in multi-ethnic London*. Cambridge: Cambridge University Press.

Bayart, J. (2005). *The illusion of cultural identity*. London: C. Hurst & Co.

Bennett, M. (1986). A developmental approach to training for intercultural sensitivity. *International Journal of Intercultural Relations*, *10*(2), 179–195.

Bensa, A. (2010). *Après Lévi-Strauss pour une anthropologie à taille humaine*. Paris: Éd. Textuel.

Benvenuto, S. (2020). Welcome to seclusion. Retrieved September 20, 2020 from www.journal-psychoanalysis.eu/coronavirus-and-philosophers/

Berdyaev, N. (1960). *The destiny of man*. New York: Harper.

Berdyaev, N. (1962). *Truth and revelation*. New York: Collier Books.

Bergson, H. (1911). *Laughter: An essay on the meaning of the comic*. København: Green Integer.

Bergson, H. (1946). *The creative mind*. New York: Philosophical Library.

Bergson, H. (2002). *Key writings*. London: Bloomsbury Academic.

Billetier, J.-F. (n.d.). Interpreting China for the West–Jean François Billeter. Retrieved September 18, 2020 from www.youtube.com/watch?v=cthAXVJuu_Y

Boulez, P. (1996). *Conversations with Boulez: Thoughts on conducting*. Bradford: Amadeus Press.

Bouveresse, J. (2008). *La connaissance de l'écrivain: Sur la littérature, la vérité & la vie*. Marseille: Agone.

Breidenbach, J., & Nyíri, P. (2005). *China inside out contemporary Chinese nationalism and transnationalism*. Budapest, Hungary & New York, NY: Central European University Press.

Byram, M. (1997). *Teaching and assessing intercultural communicative competence*. Bristol: Multilingual Matters.

Byram, M. (2020). The responsibilities of language teachers when teaching intercultural competence and citizenship: An essay. *China Media Research*, *16*(2), 77–84.

Cage, J., & Goldberg, J. (1976). John Cage: Interviewed by Jeff Goldberg. *The Transatlantic Review*, *55/56*, 103–110.

Cassin, B. (2016). Translation as paradigm for human sciences. *The Journal of Speculative Philosophy*, *30*(3), 242–266. doi:10.5325/jspecphil.30.3.0242

Chauvier, É. (2017). *Anthropologie de l'ordinaire: Une conversion du regard*. Toulouse: Anarchasis.

Cheng, A. (2014). *Histoire de la pensée chinoise*. Paris: Éd. Points.

Cheng, A. (2016). La Chine, éternelle "Autre" de l'Europe? [video]. Retrieved from www.youtube.com/watch?v=LxlFtN9HcWM&t=2939s

Christie, A. (1923). *The murder on the links*. London: Penguin Classics.

Cioran, É. (1985). *Drawn and quartered*. New York: Seaver Books.

Council of Europe. (2018a). *Reference framework for democratic culture: Volume one: Contexts, concepts and model*. Strasbourg: Council of Europe Publishing.

Council of Europe. (2018b). *Reference framework for democratic culture: Volume two: Descriptors of competences for democratic culture.* Strasbourg: Council of Europe Publishing.

Council of Europe. (2018c). *Reference framework for democratic culture: Volume three: Guidance for implementation.* Strasbourg: Council of Europe Publishing.

Dabashi, H. (2015). *Can non-Europeans think?* London: Zed Books.

Deleuze, G. (1990). *The logic of sense* (trans. M. Lester & C. Stivale). London: Athlone.

Deleuze, G. (1994). *Difference and repetition.* New York: Columbia University Press.

Deleuze, G. (1995). *Negotiations, 1972–1990.* New York: Columbia University Press.

Deleuze, G., & Guattari, F. (1980). *A thousand plateaus: Capitalism and schizophrenia* (trans. B. Massumi). Minneapolis: University of Minnesota Press.

Demoule, J.-P. (2017). *Mais où sont passés les Indo-Européens? Le mythe d'origine de l'Occident.* Paris: Points.

Dervin, F. (2011). A plea for change in research on intercultural discourses: A "liquid" approach to the study of the acculturation of Chinese students. *Journal of Multicultural Discourses, 6*(1), 37–52. https://doi.org/10.1080/17447143.2010.532218

Dervin, F. (2013). *La meilleure éducation au monde?* Paris: L'Harmattan.

Dervin, F. (2016a). *Interculturality in education: A theoretical and methodological toolbox.* London: Palgrave Macmillan.

Dervin, F. (2016b). Is the emperor naked? Experiencing the "PISA hysteria", branding and education export in Finnish academia. In Trimmer, K. (Ed.), *Political pressures on educational and social research: International perspectives* (pp. 77–93). London: Routledge.

Dervin, F. (2019a). 《破解神话：还原真实的芬兰教育》：破解神话：还原真实的芬兰教育. Beijing: MoveableType.

Dervin, F. (2020). Creating and combining models of intercultural competence for teacher education/training: On the need to rethink IC frequently. In Dervin, F., Moloney, R., & Simpson, A. (Eds.), *Intercultural competence in the work of teachers: Confronting ideologies and practices* (pp. 57–72). Abingdon, Oxon: Routledge.

Dervin, F., & Auger, N. (Eds.). (2012). *Pour une didactique des imaginaires dans l'enseignement-apprentissage des langues étrangères.* Paris: L'Harmattan.

Dervin, F., Chen, N., Yuan, M., Sude, & Jacobsson, A. (2020). COVID-19 and interculturality: First lessons for teacher educators. *Education and Society, 38*(1), 89–106. https://doi.org/10.7459/es/38.1.06

Dervin, F., Gajardo, A., & Lavanchy, A. (2013). *Politics of interculturality.* Newcastle: Cambridge Scholars.

Dervin, F., & Jacobsson, A. (2020). *Teacher education for critical and reflexive interculturality.* London: Palgrave Macmillan.

Dervin, F., & Machart, R. (2015). *Cultural essentialism in intercultural relations.* London, UK: Palgrave Macmillan.

Dervin, F., & Machart, R. (2017). *Intercultural communication with China: Beyond (reverse) essentialism and culturalism?* Singapore: Springer.

124    *Bibliography*

Dervin, F., & Simpson, A. (2019). Transnational edu-business in China: A case study of culturalist market-making from Finland. *Frontiers of Education in China, 14*(1), 33–58. https://doi.org/10.1007/s11516-019-0002-z

Diderot, D. (1773/2014). *The paradox of the actor*. Ulsan: University of Ulsan Press.

Dobzhansky, T. (1950). The genetic basis of evolution. *Scientific American, 182*(1), 32–41.

Dostoevsky, F. (2001). *The idiot*. New York: Vintage Books.

Ducrot, O. (2018). *Dire et ne pas dire: Principes de sémantique linguistique*. Paris: Hermann.

Dwivedi, D., & Mohan, S. (2020). The community of the forsaken: A response to Agamben and Nancy. Retrieved September 20, 2020 from www.journal-psychoanalysis.eu/on-pandemics-nancy-esposito-nancy/

Eriksen, T. H. (2001a). Between universalism and relativism: A critique of the UNESCO concept of culture. *Culture and Rights*, 127–148. doi:10.1017/cbo9780511804687.008

Eriksen, T. H. (2001b). *Small places, large issues: An introduction to social and cultural anthropology*. London: Pluto Press.

Esposito, R. (2008). *Bios: Biopolitics and philosophy*. Minneapolis: University of Minnesota Press.

Esposito, R. (2009). *Communitas: The origin and destiny of community* (trans. T. Campbell). Stamford: Stamford University Press.

Esposito, R. (2012). *The third person: Politics of life and philosophy of the impersonal* (trans. Z. Hanafi). London: Polity Press.

Esposito, R. (2017). *The origin of the political: Hannah Arendt or Simone Weil?* New York: Fordham University Press.

Esposito, R. (2020). Vitam instituere. Retrieved September 20, 2020 from www.journal-psychoanalysis.eu/vitam-instituere/

Etymonline.com. (2020). Respect. Retrieved September 20, 2020 from www.etymonline.com/search?q=respect

Fang, W. (2019). *Modern notions of civilization and culture in China*. Beijing: Springer.

Farber, P. L. (2016). Dobzhansky and Montagu's debate on race: The aftermath. *Journal of the History of Biology, 49*(4), 625–639.

Fitzpatrick, F. (2017). Taking the "culture" out of "culture shock": A critical review of literature on cross-cultural adjustment in international relocation. *Critical Perspectives on International Business, 13*(4), 278–296. https://doi.org/10.1108/cpoib-01-2017-0008

Flaubert, G. (1989). *A sentimental education: The story of a young man*. Oxford: Oxford University Press.

Foucault, M. (1997). *The politics of truth*. New York: Semiotext.

Gannett, L. (2013). Theodosius Dobzhansky and the genetic race concept. *Studies in History and Philosophy of Science Part C: Studies in History and Philosophy of Biological and Biomedical Sciences, 44*(3), 250–261.

Gaultier, J. de. (1902). *Bovarysme*. Paris: Mercure de France.

Gillespie, A. (2006). *Becoming other: From social interaction to self-reflection*. Greenwich: IAP-Information Age Publ.

Gluck, C., & Lowenhaupt Tsing, A. (Eds.). (2009). *Words in motion: Toward a global lexicon*. Durham & London: Duke University Press.

Goldstein, H. (2004). International comparisons of student attainment: Some issues arising from the PISA study. *Assessment in Education: Principles, Policy and Practice, 11*, 319–330.

Goodrich, P. (1997). Hermes and institutional structures: An essay on dogmatic communication. In Goodrich, P. (Ed.), *Law and the unconscious: Language, discourse, society* (pp. 137–163). London: Palgrave Macmillan.

Goody, J. (2006). *The theft of history*. Cambridge: Cambridge University Press.

Grek, S. (2009). Governing by numbers: The PISA "effect" in Europe. *Journal of Education Policy, 24*(1), 23–37. doi:10.1080/02680930802412669

Guo, X. (2008). *A concise Chinese-English dictionary for lovers*. London: Vintage Books.

Guo, X. (2020). *A lover's discourse*. London: Vintage.

Hall, E. T. (1959). *The silent language*. New York: Anchor Books.

Hall, E. T., & Trager, G. L. (1953). *The analysis of culture*. New York: American Council of Learned Societies.

Hannerz, U. (1996). *Transnational connections: Culture, people, places*. London: Routledge.

Hansen, M. H., & Svarverud, R. (Eds.). (2010). *iChina: The rise of the individual in modern Chinese society*. Copenhagen: NIAS Press.

Hansen, V. (2020). *The year 1000: When explorers connected the world and globalization began*. New York: Scribner.

Hinrichsen, J., Lange, J., & Reichel, R. (Eds.). (2020). *Diversities: Theories & practices: Festschrift for Reinhard Johler*. Tübingen: Untersuchungen des Ludwig-Uhland-Instituts der Universität Tübingen.

Hofstede, G. (1983). National cultures in four dimensions: A research-based theory of cultural differences among nations. *International Studies of Management & Organization, 13*(1–2), 46–74.

Holliday, A., Hyde, M., & Kullman, J. (2010). *Intercultural communication: An advanced resource book for students*. London: Routledge.

Horvat, S. (2019). *Poetry from the future: Why a global liberation movement is our civilisation's last chance*. London: Penguin Classics.

Hui, T., & Dervin, F. (forthcoming). "I feel somehow, all as human, we are all the same": Students' perception and construction of interculturality in China. Journal of Bilingual Education and Bilingualism.

Jankélévitch, V., & Berlowitz, B. (1978). *Quelque part dans l'inachevé*. Paris: Gallimard.

Kerbrat-Orecchioni, C. (2014). *L'énonciation: De la subjectivité dans le langage*. Paris: Armand Colin.

Kliger, I. (2008). Heroic aesthetics and modernist critique: Extrapolations from Bakhtin's author and hero in aesthetic activity. *Slavic Review, 67*(3), 551–566.

Kraus, K. (2014). *In these great times*. Amsterdam: November Editions.

Laing, R. D. (1969). *The divided self: A study of sanity and madness*. London: Tavistock.

Lakoff, R. (1992). *Talking power: The politics of language*. New York: Basic Books.

Lao, S. (1929). *Mr ma & son*. London: Penguin Classics.

Lao, S. (2014). *Mr Ma and son*. London: Penguin Classics.

Lavanchy, A., Gajardo, A., & Dervin, F. (2014). *Anthropologies de l'interculturalité*. Paris: L'Harmattan.

Leeds-Hurwitz, W. (2014). Intercultural dialogue. *Key Concepts in Intercultural Dialogue*, 1. Retrieved from https://centerforinterculturaldialogue.files.wordpress.com/2014/02/key-concept-intercultural-dialogue1.pdf

Lefort, C. (2007). *Complications: Communism and the dilemmas of democracy*. New York: Columbia University Press.

Lévinas, E. (1985). *Ethics and infinity*. Karnataka: Claretian Publications.

Lewis, R. (2004). *Finland, cultural Lone Wolf*. Boston, MA: Nicholas Brealey Publishing.

Ling, Z. (2020). *À l'origine*. Retrieved from www.enfantdimmigrcs.fr

Linhart, D. (2015). *La comédie humaine du travail: De la déshumanisation taylorienne à la sur-humanisation managériale*. Toulouse: Érès.

Lönnrot, E. (1894). *Kalevala*. Helsinki: Suomalaisen kirjallisuuden seuran kirjapainossa.

Lukács, G. (2010). *Soul and form*. New York: Columbia University Press.

Machart, R., Dervin, F., & Gao, M. (2016). *Intercultural masquerade: New orientalism, new occidentalism, old exoticism*. Heidelberg: Springer.

Maffesoli, M. (1996). *The time of the tribes*. London: Sage.

Maffesoli, M. (2020). La crise du coronavirus ou le grand retour du tragique [The coronavirus crisis or the return of the tragic]. *Le Figaro*, March 23. Retrieved from www.lefigaro.fr/vox/societe/michel-maffesoli-la-crise-du-coronavirus-ou-le-grand-retour-du-tragique-20200323

Malraux, A. (1967). *Antimemoirs*. London: Hamish Hamilton.

Mantel, H. (2009). The way to glory. *London Review of Books*, *10*(5). Retrieved from www.lrb.co.uk/the-paper/v10/n05/hilary-mantel/the-way-to-glory

Markova, I., Linell, P., Grossen, M., & Salazar Orvig, A. (2007). *Dialogue in focus groups: Exploring socially shared knowledge*. London: Equinox Publishing.

Marnette, S. (2005). *Speech and thought presentation in French: Concepts and strategies*. Amsterdam: John Benjamins Publishing.

Mok, E. (2020). What would you say I am? *From The Rooftops: A Showcase of East Asian Talent*, July 17. Retrieved from https://readingfringefestival.co.uk/whats-on/from-the-rooftops-a-showcase-of-east-asian-talent/

Mouffe, C. (2005). *On the political*. London: Routledge.

Mouffe, C. (2013). *Agonistics: Thinking the world politically*. London: Verso.

Musil, R. (1994). *Precision and soul: Essays and addresses*. Chicago: University of Chicago Press.

Musil, R. (1996). *The man without qualities*. New York: Vintage Books.

Nancy, J. L. (1991). *The inoperative community*. Minneapolis: University of Minnesota Press.

Nelson, E. S. (2019). *Chinese and buddhist philosophy in early twentieth-century german thought*. London: Bloomsbury Academic.

Niemi, H., Toom, A., & Kallioniemi, A. (2016). *Miracle of education: The principles and practices of teaching and learning in Finnish schools*. Rotterdam: Sense.

Ogay, T., & Edelmann, D. (2016). "Taking culture seriously": Implications for intercultural education and training. *European Journal of Teacher Education, 39*(3), 388–400. doi:10.1080/02619768.2016.1157160

Paveau, M. (2006). *Les prédiscours*. S.l.: Presses Sorbonne Nouvelle.

Perkins, F. (2004). *Leibniz and China: A commerce of light*. Cambridge: Cambridge University Press.

Phillips, A. (2007). *Multiculturalism without culture*. Princeton, NJ: Princeton University Press.

Pieterse, J. N. (2004). *Globalization and culture: Global mélange*. Lanham, MD: Rowman & Littlefield.

Piller, I. (2010). *Intercultural communication*. Edinburgh: Edinburgh University Press.

Popper, K. (2002). *Unended quest: An intellectual autobiography*. London: Routledge.

Qu, W. (2020). Can China's distinctive academic niches go to the world? *Contemporary Foreign Language Research*. Retrieved from https://mp.weixin. qq.com/s/61dul86LBebN6n_X-pY-Gw

R'boul, H. (forthcoming). Postcolonial interventions in intercultural communication knowledge: Meta-intercultural ontologies, decolonial knowledges and epistemological polylogue. *Journal of International and Intercultural Communication*.

Rendall, S. (2014). Culture. In Cassin, B., Apter, E., Lezra, J., & Wood, M. (Eds.), *Dictionary of untranslatables: A philosophical lexicon* (p. 191). Princeton, NJ: Princeton University Press.

Riitaoja, A.-L., & Dervin, F. (2014). Interreligious dialogue in schools: Beyond asymmetry and categorisation? *Language and Intercultural Communication, 14*(1), 76–90. doi:10.1080/14708477.2013.866125

Ronchi, R. (2020). The virtues of the virus. Retrieved September 20, 2020 from www.journal-psychoanalysis.eu/on-pandemics-nancy-esposito-nancy/

Roucek, J. S. (1944). A history of the concept of ideology. *Journal of the History of Ideas, 5*(4), 479–488. doi:10.2307/2707082

Roulet, E. (1991). *L'Articulation du discours en français contemporain*. Berne: P. Lang.

Sahlberg, P. (2011). *Finnish lessons: What can the world learn from educational change in Finland?* New York: Teachers College Press.

Said, E. W. (1996). *Representations of the intellectual: The 1993 Reith lectures*. New York: Vintage Books.

Salinger, J. D. (1958). *The catcher in the rye*. Harmondsworth: Penguin Books in association with Hamish Hamilton.

Sartre, J. (1964). *Being and nothingness: An essay in phenomenological ontology*. New York: Citadel Press.

Sen, A. (2007). *Identity and violence: The illusion of destiny*. London: Penguin Classics.

Sidorkin, A. M. (1999). *Beyond discourse: Education, the self, and dialogue*. New York: SUNY Press.

Simpson, A., Chen, N., & Dervin, F. (2019). Finnish professors' experiences of decolonisation and internationalisation in South African universities. *Education and Society, 37*(2), 5–24. Retrieved from www.ingentaconnect.com/contentone/jnp/es/2019/00000037/00000002/art00002

Simpson, A., & Dervin, F. (2019a). The Council of Europe Reference Framework of Competences for Democratic Culture: Ideological refractions, othering and obedient politics. *Intercultural Communication Education, 2*(3), 102–119. https://doi.org/10.29140/ice.v2n3.168

Simpson, A., & Dervin, F. (2019b). Forms of dialogism in the Council of Europe Reference Framework on Competences for Democratic Culture. *Journal of Multilingual and Multicultural Development, 41*(4), 305–319.

Simpson, A., & Dervin, F. (2019c). Global and intercultural competences for whom? By whom? For what purpose?: An example from the Asia society and the OECD. *Compare: A Journal of Comparative and International Education, 49*(4), 672–677. https://dx.doi.org/10.1080/03057925.2019.1586194

Simpson, A., & Dervin, F. (2019d). 走向注重对话与伦理的跨文化交际教育: 来自两位"边缘"人物的启示. 跨文化研究论丛（半年刊, *1*(1), 14–30.

Singer, P. (1980). *Marx: A very short introduction.* Oxford: Oxford University Press.

Solovyov, V. S. (1965). *Foundations of theoretical philosophy* (trans. V. Tolley & J. P. Scanlan). Chicago: University of Chicago Press.

Stasavage, D. (2020). *The decline and rise of democracy: A global history from antiquity to today.* Princeton, NJ: Princeton University Press.

St Exupéry, A. de (1943/1971). *The little prince.* San Diego, USA: Harcourt, Brace and World, Inc.

Stiegler, B. (2015). *States of shock: Stupidity and knowledge in the twenty-first century.* Cambridge: Polity Press.

Stiegler, B. (2019). *"Il faut s'adapter": Sur un nouvel impératif politique.* Paris: Gallimard.

Subrahmanyam, S. (2011). *Three ways to be Alien.* Hanover: Brandeis University Press.

Sude, Yuan, M., & Dervin, F. (2020). *Introduction to ethnic minority education in China: Policies and practices.* Frankfurt: Springer-Verlag Berlin An.

Sue, D. W. (2010). *Microaggressions in everyday life: Race, gender, and sexual orientation.* Hoboken, NJ: John Wiley and Sons.

Valéry, P. (1943). *Tel quel.* Paris: Gallimard.

Valéry, P. (1958). *The art of poetry.* London: Routledge and Paul.

Vasylchenko, A. (2014a). Postupok. In Cassin, B., Apter, E., Lezra, J., & Wood, M. (Eds.), *Dictionary of untranslatables: A philosophical lexicon* (pp. 811–812). Princeton: Princeton University Press.

Vasylchenko, A. (2014b). Svoboda. In Cassin, B., Apter, E., Lezra, J., & Wood, M. (Eds.), *Dictionary of untranslatables: A philosophical lexicon* (pp. 1105–1108). Princeton: Princeton University Press.

Vasylchenko, A. (2014c). Istina. In Cassin, B., Apter, E., Lezra, J., & Wood, M. (Eds.), *Dictionary of untranslatables: A philosophical lexicon* (pp. 513–515). Princeton: Princeton University Press.

Voloshinov, V. N. (1973a). *Marxism and the philosophy of language* (trans. I. R. Titunik & L. Matejka). Cambridge: Harvard University Press.

Voloshinov, V. N. (1973b). *Marxism and the philosophy of language* (trans. L. Matejka & I. R. Titunik). New York: Seminar Press.

Weber, M. (1949). *The methodology of the social sciences.* New York: The Free Press of Glencoe.

Wikan, U. (2002). *Generous betrayal: Politics of culture in the new Europe.* Chicago: University of Chicago Press.

Xiao, Q. (2010). *Traveller without a map.* Nanjing: Jiangsu Literature and Art Publishing House.

Yuan, M., Sude, & Tao, J. (2019). 新时代民族教育的应然价值关照. 教育研究, *10*, 102–108.

Yuan, M., Sude, Wang, T., Zhang, W., Chen, N., Simpson, A., & Dervin, F. (2020). Chinese Minzu education in higher education: An inspiration for "Western" diversity education? *British Journal of Educational Studies, 68*(4), 461–486. doi:10.1 080/00071005.2020.1712323

Yuxin, J., Byram, M., Xuerui, J., Li, S., and Xuerui, J. (2019). *Experiencing global intercultural communication: Preparing for a community of shared future for mankind and global citizenship.* Beijing: BFSU Press.

Zhuangzi. (2013). *The complete works of Zhuangzi.* New York: Columbia University Press.

# Index

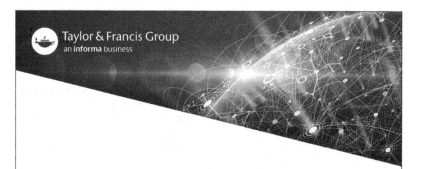

Printed in the United States
by Baker & Taylor Publisher Services